I0171920

Spectral Realms

No. 16 ‡ Winter 2022

Edited by S. T. Joshi

The spectral realms that thou canst see
With eyes veil'd from the world and me.

H. P. LOVECRAFT, "To a Dreamer"

SPECTRAL REALMS is published twice a year by Hippocampus Press,
P.O. Box 641, New York, NY 10156 (www.hippocampuspress.com).
Cover art: A *Witches' Sabbath* by Cornelis Saftleven, c. 1650.
Cover design by Daniel V. Sauer, dansauerdesign.com
Hippocampus Press logo by Anastasia Damianakos.

ISBN 978-1-61498-360-6   ISSN 2333-4215

Contents

Poems 5

Acid Rain / Ngo Binh Anh Khoa 7

Father's Bullet: A Tale of the Apocalypse / Carl E. Reed 8

Lenore to Her Tragic Muse, Edgar Allan Poe / Adele Gardner 10

Medusa / Christina Sng 12

The King of Cats / Adam Bolivar 13

The Great Parade / Maxwell I. Gold 14

Date Night / Melissa Ridley Elmes 15

The Pillarist of Leptis Magna / Manuel Pérez-Campos 16

Otherworld / Lori R. Lopez 18

The Bog-Track / Ann K. Schwader 21

Children of the Night / DJ Tyrer 22

Saith the Witch / Wade German 23

The Clingers / Frank Coffman 24

In the Graveyard, Decomposing / LindaAnn LoSchiavo 25

The Flotsam of Want / Claire Smith 26

Star Dust / Geoffrey Reiter 27

Betrayed / Christine Irving 28

A Frosty Love / Charles Lovecraft 30

The Mad Scientist's Assistant / Darrell Schweitzer 31

Gray Grimalkin / Scott J. Couturier 32

Altagracia's Lament / Manuel Arenas 34

Water Slave / Harris Coverley 36

The Unlocking / David Barker 37

Incubus / P. B. Grant 38

My Sweetheart's Name Is Despair / John Shirley 39

Tonight's Tale: Devil County, USA / Mack W. Mani 40

Palazzo San Felice / Benjamin Blake 43

River Dweller / Jordan Zuniga 44

We Met in No-Man's-Land / Carl E. Reed 45

Bone-Taster / Thomas Goff 49

Mukkelevi / Melissa Ridley Elmes 50

Ealren Halgena Æfen / Wade German 52

Infernal Carnival / Ngo Binh Anh Khoa 53

The Harvest Reaped and Threshed / Oliver Smith 56

All Fires Light the Wicker Man / Scott J. Couturier 58

Zombie Moon / Margaret Curtis 60

Eidolon Tetratych / Frank Coffman 62

Written in Smoke / Ann K. Schwader 66

The Beast with a Billion Stomachs / Maxwell I. Gold 67

The Whippoorwill / Lori R. Lopez..68

Digging Beneath the Battlefield / Steven Withrow 72

The Dark Sorcerer / Charles Lovecraft 74

On Finding the Man / Holly Day..75

As the Dream Descends / Kurt Newton 76

The Poltergeists of Park Slope / LindaAnn LoSchiavo.......................78

City of Carrion, Valley of Darkness / Harris Coverley.......................80

Hand of Glory / Manuel Arenas 82

In a Haunted Holler / Adam Bolivar 83

Lines on the Mistress of an Old Sea-Town / Manuel Pérez-Campos ..84

Those That We Meet in Dark Country Lanes / Darrell Schweitzer ...85

The God of Dark Fantasy Prose-Poetry / Jay Sturner 86

Aubade / Paul Grant...88

Starfall / Melissa Ridley Elmes 89

The Mimics / Christina Sng 90

Gilgamesh in Mourning / Geoffrey Reiter...93

The King in Yellow / Ngo Binh Anh Khoa 94

The Dominion of the Son of the Dragon / Jordan Zuniga 95

City of Dreams / Maxwell I. Gold 96

The Outsider / Carl E. Reed 97

Zwartenberg the Necromancer / Manuel Arenas................................98

Our Last Halloween / Adele Gardner...100

Crypt Currency / Wade German 102

The Pixie-Ring / Scott J. Couturier 103

Serenade for Black Plague Gwynneth / Manuel Pérez-Campos 104

The Lorelei / Frank Coffman 106

Classic Reprints... 107

   Beside the Dead / Ina Coolbrith 109

   The Pearl / Henry Anderson Lafler..110

Reviews... 117

   Born under Saturn Indeed / Donald Sidney-Fryer 119

   Phantasmascope / Donald Sidney-Fryer...123

Notes on Contributors.. 129

Poems

Acid Rain

Ngo Binh Anh Khoa

A raindrop from the suddenly dark sky falls,
A slobbery splatter splashing on my cheek,
And starts a torrent that exudes a reek
Into the rumbling air suffused with calls
For help. Then come shocked cries of agony
From panicking people blindly running round
Like rattled ants that flee a flooding mound,
Their sodden flesh corroding rapidly.

I clutch my burning face and strive to hide
In vain as buildings melt. My scream's among
The countless in a frenzied, anguished song
With scores of terrors in time magnified—
Which hits a shrill crescendo when we spy
A salivating maw that dims the sky.

Father's Bullet: A Tale of the Apocalypse

Carl E. Reed

It is the pastel-colored
swirling rainbow
unicorn dress
& glittering zircon tiara
that first catches my eye
daughter
when I spot you
stumbling amongst them.

I track your body through the 10X scope—
tremor in the hands; water in the eye.
Deep breath—
    hold—
        partial exhale.
A light caress of the trigger
& the rifle bucks against my shoulder—

Your face at your eighth birthday party:
how you
shone with love & joy
bent low over cake & candles,
drew in breath—

*   *   *

—the .300 grain Winchester magnum bullet
blows out your brains
stops
your idiot moaning & shuffling
in the front rank
of that
oncoming
slack-jawed horde.

Lenore to Her Tragic Muse, Edgar Allan Poe

(19 January 1809–7 October 1849)
In Answer to His Own "The Raven"

Adele Gardner

Once within the drear October, days I scarcely dare remember,
Still believing that the faith of one could conquer fatal woe,
Messenger arrived most evil, letter penned by drink or devil,
News about my love primeval, dead forever—Edgar Poe!
Alas, my tragic, lost, forlorn, beloved Edgar Allan Poe!
                  Yowled the black cat, "Let him go!"

How might maiden part the curtain, slip behind to view his burden,
Find the secret source of hurt that answered happiness with "No"?
And how live with this dark mischief, cat as black as Satan's kerchief,
Bringing me the word I purchased without heed for cost or woe—
My lover's heart, subsumed by grief for one he loved, now ash and woe—
                  Yowled the black cat, "Let him go!"

Still I hung, dazed maiden martyr—with each tug clung tighter, harder,
To that rope which deep into the awful Stygian grave did go—
"Love," I gasped, "let loose the curtain—show your heart, howe'er
    uncertain—
Take me not into the grave by way of parcelling your woe—
From this grim portion spare the maid who unto death doth love you
    so—"
                  Yowled the black cat, "Let him go!"

Then I spied stones cast asunder, crumbled by some deadly thunder,
As though grief propelled the sleeper to cast off the name of Poe—
Step out of the tomb that carried ghosts of all the loved and buried,
Mother, bride, his own name storied, world-renowned Edgar A. Poe—
How I pined for my own lost and tragic Edgar Allan Poe—
                    Yowled the black cat, "Let him go!"

In a dream that stole my senses, dark as Edgar's hair and lenses
Of his soul, those dearest eyes that ever let love's true tears flow,
So he wept for wife and mother—so weep I, 'fianced no longer,
To that tender soul whose squandered secrets went to grave below,
Heart so tender there to fester in that self-dug grave below—
                    Yowled the black cat, "Let him go!"

"No!" I cried. "I love forever! Spin me out no tales of censure,
Stories of the ladies swooning to the voice of Edgar Poe,
Still declaiming, still declaiming, in his ringing voice, that Raven
Who rends still my heart—with claws now, in his cat-shape, sly and low,
A witchy, slinky shape of omen, growls sepulchral, hollow—No!"
                    Yowled the black cat, "Let him go!"

"I cannot! I shall haunt eternal that lost heart, to keep it vernal!
Poe lives on in me, e'en should his shade have nowhere else to go!"
But the black cat chuckled, prowling, with scoring claws, unearthly
     yowling,
Demanded I pay heed to one foul note I'd rather burn than know:
Words my pining lover wrote when of my breath he did not know—
                    Die not for me, my Edgar Poe!

Medusa

Christina Sng

Medusa slithers
Through the hallway,
Her snakes on alert,
Darting.

She's been searching
All over Sarpedon
For her lovey Petunia
That Momma gave her

Last year
For her 11th birthday—
The only thing remaining
She won't turn to stone.

The King of Cats

Adam Bolivar

In a wild wood,   where witches meet
And ravens roost   in rowan trees,
I came across   an uncanny scene
In remote ruins,   rotted by years—
A cavalcade of cats,   a coffin on their backs,
A crown upon   the casket's lid,
Strode softly by   with solemn dignity.
Raving, I ran   rapidly homeward
Where my wife wondered   at my worried looks.
I told her my tale   and Tom, my cat,
Who was sleeping soundly   by the sparking fire
Jumped up jubilantly   and jigged on hind legs.
"Now I am King of Cats!"   he cried with glee.
And vaulted up the chimney,   vanishing forevermore.

The Great Parade

Maxwell I. Gold

Drumming over the tired earth, hoofbeats and horrors rammed through the rusted gates of Hell, blasting forth from the hungry nethers, wild music of bedlam and dread. Gaping abysms yawned with new vigor from weak fissures in the dying planet as fire and death leaked into boiling oceans, collapsing the skies into an ashy, acidic embrace. Volcanic bursts as if dying laughter, covered the world in molten indifference, swallowing civilizations in slow, deliberate orchestrations when suddenly, rising through the hot liquid rubescence; a dreadful parade of monsters; daemons, dybbuks, trolls and goblins, viruses, vagabonds, and witches rose from the Stygian black depths. Dancing to the new music of pixels and pocket gods, polluting the air in darkness and doom, the last remnant cities saw their streets cluttered with cackling witches, lumbering Cyclopes, and slithery dimensional beings, waning in the shadowy fog of a broken portal on the most profane night of all. The end of all nights, the beginning of an existence where monsters saw the tired earth under hoofbeat and horror, dismantling the Old Horned God's rusty gate leaving him trapped in a bottomless lake of burning ice, unable to revel and dance in the flamboyance of a new world; unable to march in the parade of monsters. Drumming over the tired earth, where daemons, dybbuks, trolls and goblins sang, billowing clouds of brimstone and soot frothed into the highest pillars, charring the stars themselves. Drumming over the tired earth, the parade of monsters blasted wild music of bedlam and dread.

Date Night

Melissa Ridley Elmes

When the moonlight parts the mists,
When the veil between realms thins,
When the faeries gather in the glen,
Meet me at the water's edge—
And we'll swim across the worlds.

The Pillarist of Leptis Magna

Manuel Pérez-Campos

Austere and accursed and laden with antiquity,
the nacarat sand under a sky sieged by bolides
and a hellfire bringer six-tailed comet as though
to escape its undiminished desolation keeps
inventing detours of extended gyre: it is here
that the flickering shells of self-luminous specters

attired in obsolescent rags moaning sotto voce
blow about, too overly enervated by their gradual
assimilation into the aeons to bother wayfarers:
and it is here, where all from bent royal palm tree
to desiccated artesian well is under counsel
of insinuant wind and ubiquitous sun that I came

to bind my soul to the colossal disrepair of Leptis
Magna, that outpost port hustle of oppressive
trade, purveyor of exotica to the Colosseum
and patrician parlours of Rome, for Rome to toy
with and destroy, its pomp—prefigured from
massive pediments of xanthic sheen by panpipe

of wild-haired satyrs ensnared in the coils
of a sea serpent—impassive despite vivific mud
during sea storm season but which is now long
past the stuff of gossip because a complex
merely of desultory isolated walls and arches
amid a palimpsest pile of heat-tarnished marble

shards (bristling in their depths with the irascible
helter-skelter of scorpions but which if charily
sifted can still flash out the triumphal crescendo
of kitharas to which summoned ghawazees once
swayed in palace penetralia or the thrush-allayed
silence of courtyards lined with wispy statuary

in stola of wide-eyed Juturna, protectress of
fountain rainbows) and thus indulge in the illusion
of an intermission from living: I became half-naked,
and as unaccomplished and squalid as a beast:
and with unprecedented resolve crouched on
the tall stump of a fluted limestone pillar cracked

by lichen and black fungi that stuck out of sunken
stylobate like a wan reminder of erstwhile ambition
to oversee without time-limit the wretchedness
of this great nothing: and at length came to sense
that I was cloistered in a precinct beyond
the haze of dreams, utterly odious in its raw reality.

Otherworld

Lori R. Lopez

The body stood in the road, facing traffic,
stiff as a bronze statue without a pedestal.
Awkward of stance. Displaced on the street.
A fellow in a robe, gray sweatpants, a T-shirt.
Why did he stop there? Was he skirting the
clamor of the Founder's Day Celebration like me?
Shy of crowds, I only went for the free stuff.

Considering his behavior, I decided my proper
course of action: to inquire if he required assistance.
The answer seemed obvious, unnecessary. Asking
would force me to step outside the polite sphere
of a quiet, minimal-interaction, go-about-my-business
routine and actually get involved. That was for heroes.
Outgoing types. I preferred nods; an occasional smile.

Clearing my throat, approaching on hesitant feet,
I could tell from less distance the man's visage
had an unnatural shade, kind of greenish-orange
like unripe fruit. Weird. Maybe contagious.
I backed away, not speaking. His orbs blinked
at sluggish intervals. Everything about him
freakishly off, I retreated in haste. A coward.

More of them appeared. Peculiar sentinels.
Random statues paused here and there as if
glued to the ground, frozen in the midst of a task,
a trip somewhere to do whatever. Staring.
I glimpsed them watching me from sidewalks,
porches. Through windows of houses and stores.
At the post office, an elementary school.

Otherworld, that's the term for it. Apart from
the natural realm. It was all so uncanny, unexpected.
They stopped being normal. There is something
very calming and comforting about the ordinary,
the mundane. As boring as my hometown
once appeared, I'd give anything now for its dull
inhabitants to go back to the way they were!

I started to pack. Preparing to move.
Discreetly, the curtains drawn. I couldn't risk
letting them see. Couldn't be certain what they
might do, this community of arcane motionless
observers. Full of people I knew my entire life
but no longer trust. They're not the same friends,
family, neighbors. It's scary. I'm petrified.

I feel trapped among strangers. Too late.
I fear I am changing like them. I cannot escape
turning into a silent witness. My body refuses to
obey. Thoughts match the pace of eyelids, torpid
yet keen. My gaze howls, unnoticed, unheard.
Please! There must be someone out there who
isn't stone-like. Able to act. Willing to help . . .

Who didn't drink a free cup of strawberry punch.

The Bog-Track

Ann K. Schwader

Not through the mire, but only halfway through
this neither place where earth & water meet
uneasily, its shadow on the peat
reveals a pathway. Sunken planks laid true
enough once to sustain the weight of two
(though only one returning) echo feet
both hesitant & eager to complete
the sacred task. What gods received their due
amid these mists is wisdom lost, their names
long buried with their servants—yet on nights
when moonrise whispers silver down that track
to nowhere, something answers. Wakes to claim
our nightmares, where we wander blind despite
the spectral tread of footsteps heading back.

Children of the Night

DJ Tyrer

On a couch surrounded by dreams
The Lord of Sleep reclines
Enfolded in the loving embrace
Of His mother, mighty Night
His brothers set out our fate
Leading us by the hand to Death
Along the path their sisters mark
A lifetime of Pain and Strife
Ending in the arms of Nemesis
Or Old Age
Entering the eternal Night
To whom even the Gods defer
Eldest and strongest
Yielding to the Day
Only out of love for Her daughter
Unconcerned by the raging storm
That blusters and roars
In impotent rage at Her son
Her languid favoured child
Who crafts delightful scenes
In the minds of those
She holds fast to Her breast
Or sends terrors to torment
To His sister's delight
All part of the panoply
Of the children of the Night

Saith the Witch

Wade German

All Hallows Eve, the dead from sleep emerge;
Dark forces move our dreams to strangely weave,
As mundane and the spirit world converge
    All Hallows Eve:

When ghosts shall throng unto the thaumaturge,
And demons of the outer darkness leave
Their realms for rites to raise the demiurge,

To witness incubi and witches merge
That Sabbath brides monstrosities conceive . . .
The weird night winds, like spirits, moan and surge
    All Hallows Eve . . .

The Clingers

Frank Coffman

There are souls, disembodied, and their fate—
"Denuded" from their flesh, due to foul sins
So enormous that they cannot transmigrate—
To cleave to people, so the curse begins.
People whose secret wrongs have opened *the Door*
To let "the Clinger" in. It makes them crazed.
The thing can use their mouth to speak. Before
They are aware, their body is amazed
To find two souls within! And one a *Demon* vile.
No peace for such a victim. And the schism
Between the cursed one and the *Dybbuk* soul
Grows. And the only answer—Exorcism.
    At best, into an object *the Terror* will go—
    At worst, to another human—a transferred woe.

In the Graveyard, Decomposing

LindaAnn LoSchiavo

Stealth is my friend once again. Unnoticed at lock-up time, I'm lingering
among crosses set in even rows. The gridlock of grim. Typical visitor
hours are too hectic, rife with bald human moments—slumping
shoulders mantled in misery. All the ways bereavement can scaffold joy.
A boneyard devoid of human sounds is preferable. Aware of the final,
fading pulses of light, I apostrophe myself into the dark and begin.
Crunching frost-crisped leaves underfoot produces a dry crackle like
ghosts coughing. I approach one particular monument arrayed in its
upright finery of euphemisms, letters loud with an insistence to be,
unscrew a clear solution, and begin my work. Decomposing, I become
contradiction's champion. Shedding an edge of slate, erasing a name,
obliterating the expected encomiums. Erasure pounces as acid withers
the words a line at a time, returning the stone to its gall of quiet
lovelessness. In life, he quietly murdered his first wife, dropped my
sister's corpse from his private plane like earth's least precious stone,
then kept his crimes buried by decorating his life with diplomas and
philanthropy. Her remains were never found, never graced a morgue slab
nor satin-lined coffin. But tonight I feel her spirit humming, numinous
as a melody from warped violins.

The Flotsam of Want

Claire Smith

The effluent of unearned riches leaks from my treasury;
spills under my portcullis; sprays across my moat.
Neighbouring cornfields' sprigs of growth are swept
over by murderous tides. Slicks thick with oily greed blacken
bullion, silver coins, bronze statues left as discarded scraps
on a deserted beach. The clear sea, once perfumed with salt,
is crystalised with escaped diamonds, opals, and pearls.
Centuries of dirt grow thick over crowns, chalices, sceptres.
A princess's inert body summons her killer's neck,
snapped in two, hung by a noose. Chapel-bells chime a story
of stolen blood, breath robbed, the beat of her thieved heart—
an alabaster figure left to the craft of rigor mortis.

Star Dust

Geoffrey Reiter

They say that we are made of stars, and I
Reply, "So what?" Five billion years ago
The frothing fire's primeval cosmic glow,
That chilled and scattered like the sparks that fly
From ashen embers, cooled into the sigh
Of settling atoms; molecules would grow,
Would knit to proteins, breathing life, and so
Across the aeons our cells multiply.

But what of that? A star is plasma burning,
Its slow flame dying, flaring in the deep.
If these are stars, bright mites within the dark,
How can it matter that within me, churning,
The dust of distant suns may slowly sleep
If at my last breath I can't keep their spark?

Betrayed

Christine Irving

In the pantry, she dusted clean shelves,
pulling down gaily patterned cans, wiping
a soft dust cloth across tin tops so shiny
light flew in splinters, stabbing her eye.

She had stuffed a pork loin with apricot and fig
sliding a thin sharp blade into pale pink flesh
twice, twisting the knife the second time
ninety degrees to form a cross, stuffing
the dry fruit deep toward the center of the roast
with the blunt end of her oldest wooden spoon.
Sliced, the pieces would fall like little bull's-eyes,
 juicy, black or orange, ready for an arrow.

The table sparkled, laid for two
with hand-rubbed silver, crystal glasses
frosted blue and glass Italian plates
vined in glowing leaves and holding
in their clear depths a purple droop
of delicate wisteria.

Wild mushrooms simmered in a sauce
of brandy, cream, saffron and shallots.
She'd gathered morels in the morning
still damp, new thrust from loamy beds
beneath birch, larch and sycamore

*   *   *

Digging fingers deep in crumbly earth
to break off stems beneath the soil, she'd
heaped them in her flat-bed basket
atop tangy leaves of wood sorrel
and aromatic bay.

He would eat his morels, so would she:
later they would lie down together,
make love on crisp sun-scented sheets.
She'd calculated time enough to dream
before the first spasm awoke them to what,
she fervently prayed, would be a short agony.

A Frosty Love

Charles Lovecraft

What seemed a spider's web her hair had spun.
Her blushing beauty, bluish-cast white face,
Threw vividly a frosty neon trace,
With eyes like slits of thin-edged knives side-on.
Up high, about her neck, her collar rode
Like fangs of blackened death, and which had draped
About her slender form now wrapped and caped;
Only her arms emerged. Slow lightning glowed.

The mad wind seethed around our forms. I tore
My eyes away and looked la bas, *down there,*
And reeled to see our distant feet on air
Drifting in space, the Earth as down a bore.
'Twas then she moved and sifted softly back—
And I was left alone in all that black.

The Mad Scientist's Assistant

Darrell Schweitzer

I serve him out of love,
because he loves the grotesque,
and I, who am made hideous
by nature and driven forth from mankind
in a hail of spit and stones, am surely
grotesque enough to please
such a connoisseur as my master,
who loves me in return as we
rob graves and gallows and I stand
in worshipful awe in the crackling
glare of his exaltation, trembling
in the glory of it when I am allowed
the supreme honor of, with my own hands,
throwing some of the switches,
and the thing on the table begins to move.

Yet I torment the creature he has made,
that which, grotesque, should have been my brother,
because I am afraid that he will come to love it
more than he loves me.

Gray Grimalkin

Scott J. Couturier

Gray grimalkin slinks & stalks
as Jack his All Hallows round walks,
dispensing scares & sacred frights,
grin glowing in every pumpkin's light.

Gray grimalkin likes this night
best of all: shadow-realms her right,
she rubs on skewed cemetery stones,
welcoming witches with feral moans.

Gray grimalkin sees souls rise
unquiet from graves to starry skies;
swatting at each phantom's trail,
she runs to romp in ghost-lit dales.

Gray grimalkin preens & yowls,
purrs & hisses & exalting prowls,
teeth red-stained by graveyard rats,
gore of mice & ichor of bats:

Gray grimalkin on Hallowe'en!
The eve is yours, fell feline Queen.
Take your prey as specters shock,
goblins titter & Mab's train flocks.

Gray grimalkin on Hallowe'en!
Familiar of Scratch, sly & keen!
As dawn's ray peeps she falls asleep,
reliving it all in slumbers deep.

Altagracia's Lament

Manuel Arenas

Amidst the Helldorado range, within her cavern lair
Altagracia plays a tune into the midnight air.
Tapping dolorous melodies that echo through the night;
Velvet mallets on an organ, composed of stalagmite.

Woefully wailing her sad keen into the desert night,
As the unbowed scorpion-mouse, squeals in victorious rite.
Night-blooming flowers unfurl buds in welcoming fashion,
Inviting long-nosed bats to lap their sweet nectar with passion.

Ruefully, she pines for the times before the bloodlust came:
The inborn curse which took her aunt, driving Lupe insane.
Forcing her monthly to transform, shedding her human skin
For lupine pelts and raven's wings, imbued by blood and sin.

Altagracia could not bear this curse to carry on,
And so she chose to kill her aunt, nescient of what would come.
By taking the life of Lupe, she hoped more lives to save,
But with the best of intentions the road to Hell is paved.

Tlahuelpuchi cannot be slain by one who shares their line,
The curse just passes to the kin who perpetrate the crime.
By killing Lupe, Grace took on her sanguinary bane,
Along with her occult powers, and transmogrified frame.

A vegetarian at heart, she cannot brook the thirst
For the blood of innocents, with which she has been cursed.
And fight the craving as she might, she cannot shirk her fate,
But rather acquiesce and drink until the thirst abates.

Therefore, she bays unto the moon, coyotes take her cue,
Joining in her lamentation, with guilt and gore imbrued.
Knowing that her isolation will no way stall the curse
From claiming a new-found victim with which to slake her thirst.

Wiping up tears with livid hands, her ululations spent,
She feels the change about to break as she catches a scent.
Her body writhes, her structure pops, the fur begins to spread . . .
She is now crib-death incarnate, which newborn mothers dread.

Water Slave

Harris Coverley

I entered the ship a cabin lad, and underdeck I saw him: immiserated, velvet scales of azure, his frilled and gilded finnage trailing down his neck and arms, his uniform a sack, his leg irons keeping him from anything faster than an agonised trot, dragging bags of flour and potatoes. Having seen my look of horror, the old man, at twilight over a bowl of gruel and a jar of grog, soberly advised me: "You canna change the nature of a thing, my boy. A water sprite's a treacherous devil, best left a beast o' burden." But having watched that creature in all its suffering, even less at liberty than a shanghaied and bonded rapscallion like me. . . .

And so it came as we set out on the tides to far-flung battle, I slipped from my foul hammock in the cool, oblivious night, and moved nimbly down the decks to the crevice where the petty officer allowed the sprite a place of respite. To remove his irons was a quick chore, but he absconded with the snap of the lock. As I stood there in confusion, he, without pangs or qualms, his plan long deliberated, sparked the powder store, and with the erupting roar the ship was sunk. I clung to a beam as he blithely floated by, and above the cries of men he called to me with a heinous leer: "*I cannot apologise . . . one cannot change what's in one's nature!*" And away he swam, abandoning me to providence . . . and perhaps to ponder: yes, the sprite could not change what was in his nature, but nor could the foolhardy men who had brought him on board *to begin with!*

The Unlocking

David Barker

From far-flung lands where I had sought the key
That would unlock the puzzle of the tome,
I journeyed long and found my way back home
And at my leisure solved its mystery.
The lurid text described an elder race,
Crustacean beings from Yuggoth on the rim,
Who sailed to Earth in times remote and dim
And brought the lore passed down from gods of space.

But foolish men forgot their debt to these,
Our masters from the planet Yuggoth drear
Who brought them dread sublime with ecstasies
So strong that men with glee embraced their fear.
These truths made stand erect my neck's fine hairs;
The thump of limbs upon the attic stairs!

Inspired by H. P. Lovecraft's sonnet "III. The Key" in *Fungi from Yuggoth*

Incubus

P. B. Grant

Amid the rust, disturbing dust,
She came upon his soul:
A withered sheaf of yellowed leaves
That stank of love and mold.

She took the score and sat to play:
The keys seemed sticky, slow;
But by the time she'd played his part,
Her dress was frayed and torn.

She sits there still, her heart enchained
To some forgotten poem;
And plays and weeps and plays until
Their unborn haunt her home.

My Sweetheart's Name Is Despair

John Shirley

A winsome woman of wicked curves
(Some of them are her shape)
She has no eyes, never had any
She wears only electrical tape

Dirt from our graves crusts under her nails—
blood and rust in her flaxen hair
She dances like a flag in a hurricane
My sweetheart's name is Despair

Mankind made the introduction
Charmed; it was love at first sight
Despair is my deduction
I embrace the end of light

My sweetheart's name is Despair
Rust and blood in her hair;
No hope in her eyes—nothing there
Oh my darling's name is Despair

Tonight's Tale: Devil County, USA

Mack W. Mani

In the backwoods
of Montana
there are valleys
that don't play
by the rules.

Thin zones
where entities
from other planes
ingratiate
and multiply
dividing the land
to spread the madness.

Lunatic truck bed
sledgehammer chainsaw boys.

Blood stained banner
colonies
that lie beyond
the valley beyond
The House of a Thousand Corpses.

*   *   *

People who trespass there
are never seen again,
but some have
been sent photos
of loved ones
or rarely seen reels;
images of torture
on sparkling super-8.

Women tied to porches,
prisoners from our side
marching in time,
rusty manacles
rubbing ankles raw.

So much good killing out here,
says a drawling
voice from offscreen.

Yes, rumor has it
some of us thrive there too,
right proud madmen
who've traveled
black lodge trails,
hitchhiked rides
with eldritch strangers.

*   *   *

Though some insist
we are one and the same
us and them,
but it's hard to believe
when you see them
howling slurs onscreen,
faces blistered,
drunk on bathtub gin,
twirling sacrilege
on the side
of a twilit highway.

And just beyond,
riddled with buckshot,
a message, barely visible
the signpost up ahead,
Devil County, USA.

Palazzo San Felice

Benjamin Blake

The witchcraft worked.
Working behind a makeshift altar
In an almost-empty apartment,
Housed in an eighteenth-century palace
In the failing heart of Napoli.

Tarot cards and incantations,
A lone candle burning
In the early winter evening,
The potency of harnessed maidens
And this skull-strewn city's pagan roots,
Coalesced with an antichrist
To bestow a power
That cannot be diminished
By any amount of futile prayer
Or splashings of holy water.

River Dweller

Jordan Zuniga

Shadows upon the riverbend, lurking, dwelling,
Rushing waters, waves spreading, ringing, swelling,
Upon the water's surface, the coldest breeze at night,
Monstrous in its appearance, horrid, abysmal sight,

Where once it was a habitable place for the fisherman's trade,
Now a hunting ground for the creature that preyed,
Claws like a knife's razor, webbed from grip to toe,
Slithering through the depths, where the rowers rowed,

Eyes that glowed an orange glare, slithering to what it could find,
Cautious in its judgment, shrewd as it hunted those with an absent mind,
Covered by the marsh growth, underneath the reeds,
Anxious splashes caused fear, terror scattered as seeds,

No one would dare venture, none would even dare,
To test the creature that hunted, and would sooner tear,
The monster in the coldest region, whose presence brought a shiver,
A creature in the waters, the weird hunter that dwelt within the river. . .

We Met in No-Man's-Land

Carl E. Reed

Sneak home and pray you'll never know
The hell where youth and laughter go.
—Siegfried Sassoon

Part I.

We met in no man's land, the year:
    1917;
the thunder of the guns erased
    all that stood between

two great contending armies
    twitching rat-like in the trenches;
the ripping bullet, bursting shell
    poison gas that wrenches

a bug-eyed soldier upright
    choking, clawing at his mask;
jet of hissing fuel that torches
    men who have been tasked

to flame & smoke, convulse & scream
    sizzle, red-burn, blacken—
are innocent—tools of the apes—
    planting barbed-wire bracken.

Inert the bullet, shell, & flame;
    though guilty & condemned
are the men who profit from the urge
    to kill & kill again.

Part II.

The captain asked for volunteers
    to crawl into mad hellscape:
the cratered, maggot earth
    between the trenches; only crude shapes

of tree stumps, strewn rifles,
    haversacks & rotting corpses
could be made out: grayish cloud
    obscured the moon; cold & remorseless

our stomachs clenched, balls snug-&-tight
    we met in no man's land;
taut nerves strung to fever-pitch
    sharpened blades in hand.

Two doomed patrols set out to probe
    for weakness in the lines;
colliding, fought a savage fight:
    entrenching tools & knives.

Our faces set in rictus grim
    we strove, beyond the front
to punch, & kick, & stab, & hack
    with shrieks, & oaths, & grunts.

Part III.

The Hun loomed up before me
    eyes wide-wild, white with fright;
& something more—a bayonet—
    he drove with all his might

into my birdlike chest, while I
    forced to return the favor
disemboweled him with a thrust
    & yank of knife; who braver

the German or American?
    & does it really matter?
Here, upon the killing field
    battered, bruised, blood-spattered.

We topped, he & I, together
    locked in death's embrace
into cordite-reeking shell hole
    & there, his slackening face

was pressed upon my own as he
    whimpered into my ear:
"Mütter, mütter!" The moon above
    shone bright, & cold, & clear.

Epilogue

We met in no man's land, the year:
    1917;
I, & blondish Berlin lad—
    Who knows what might have been?

Bone-Taster

Thomas Goff

I know the strangest man: his name's Bone-Taster.
He sucks at skeletal matter; discards the meat,
Except for the marrow, cracked out from within.
     A "white waster,"
A ceremonial staff, he grasps: he wields that neat
Blanched stick Elizabeth's courtiers brandished, close
By the Queen. His other Queen too brags a white face,
Lead mixed into the soft paste by which she chose
To paint young as primavera, young as grace,
Although she was and is no Elizabeth
Painting her mortal age the hue of Death,
Yet she reigns on, over even this great Bone-Taster,
Whose breath upon a man whittles him that other
     so-called White Waster.
Breathe not on me: life's far too short for the sick
Touch on my thin limbs of your fast-withering stick.

Mukkelevi

Melissa Ridley Elmes

If you saw it, you could not help but marvel
even while gripped in the throes of terror
for the most fertile of mortal imaginations
could not call such a being into existence.
The sea is full of many marvels and mysteries,
horrors and treacheries, but none so immediate
nor so malevolent as this water devil; if only he
would stay in the sea! But he does not: enraged
by human activity, he emerges from the waves
to stalk the land in the form of a man's torso
on a horse's body, arms so long the hands
can grip the ground like a gorilla's—but did
I say arms? Nay, for the whole of his body is
skinless, all you can see is the pulsing heartbeat,
black blood coursing through yellow veins, muscles
engaged in movement, sinews pulsing with the effort
as the beast lurches toward you, nothing good in its
Intentions. The head—oh, the head!—a great thing
shaped like the mouth of a pig, one fiery red eye
glaring as it makes its way inexorably toward you
hungry for human flesh; emitting a toxic vapor
that wilts the crops in its path and sickens the cows
in the fields; run, if you see it, turn and run, do not

look back, make for a freshwater loch and dive into it
with a prayer to whatever gods you pray to
to turn the evil being back into the salty waves
from whence it came; pray too it is only one, and
not joined by other horrors of the watery ocean deep.

Ealren Halgena Æfen

Wade German

WAERLOGA:
And comes the night on which we hail and host
    The spirits risen out the primal dream
Of deepest forests, where ancestral ghosts
    Attend our god and harvest his esteem—
Even as now their spectres guide our feet
    And weave the ancient darkness where we tread,
Leading upon a starlit way to greet
    The Lord: may we behold his antlered head.

WICCE:
All souls in summons of the evening know
    This night is not a time, but is a place
Between the world beyond and ours below:
    A portal on an outer, darker space,
Where all who bow their heads in reverence
    Receive a blessing of the second sight—
And shadows, guarding gates to eminence,
    Unveil the court and thrones of hallowed Night.

Infernal Carnival

Ngo Binh Anh Khoa

In Inferno, there's a place
Of delights for demon-race,
Where the sinners are condemned
For eternity without grace.

Round and round the liars go
At the carousels that show
Sinners chained to horses mad
With their flaming manes that grow
Hotter with each second past,
Scorching each undying soul.
Taken in for such a ride,
Naught but anguish they shall know.

Nearby are the stalls that sell
Endless treats and snacks quite well,
Made of eyeballs, ears and tongues
From the ones that would not tell
Others what they knew to bring
Justice to the wronged. They fell
Here, whose useless parts do make
Killer profits down in Hell.

Head inside the Central Tent
For more wonderful events
That shall make the audience wild—

Gory, glorious, violent—
Where imps juggle murderers' limbs
That are from their bodies rent
With dull blades; their conscious heads
Are toward cheering fiends then sent.

Up on thin lines walk those who
Were adulterous and would do
Risky balancing acts 'tween their
Lovers and their spouses true.
'Neath them, spikes and lava spread
To engulf or pierce them through.
Those that almost make it past
Quickly learn that fiends cheat, too.

Next come those consumed by greed,
Who committed heinous deeds,
Stealing others' properties
For themselves, they'll scream and bleed
With their arms inside the maws
Of beasts born of Mammon's seeds.
Their hands shall be crushed to naught
Ere they're felled like worthless weeds.

Battered figures bound in chains—
Victims to unceasing pains—
Are those that abused and hurt
Others, times and times again.
Dragged down here, they're helpless, trapped—
Naught but writhing, bloodied stains
Stabbed with countless throwing knives
As they wail and thrash in vain.

As for those that knew not "No,"
They, too, star in their own show,
Where they plead and plead and bleed,
Subject to unending woe.
Their cries are sweet music to
Demons that no mercy know;
No reprieve their ilk shall have
As they reap what they did sow.

There are countless more in store
For those rotten to the core
In this wicked Carnival where
Sinners die forevermore.

The Harvest Reaped and Threshed

Oliver Smith

We climbed high in the noonday sun
we reached the summit peak
and saw the world spread out below,
and weary of our endless work
we lay and took our sleep beneath
the stony skulls of giants past
eroded from the mountains rock.
We woke too late in the afternoon
and saw the darkening lens of time
dim the way between the yews,
so began our downward climb.

The broken road beneath our feet
is not the same we walked before;
the old familiar path has gone:
it winds and twists and goes too far
and takes us through outlandish realms;
the castles high, the seas so deep,
the night so broad and full of grief.
We conquered all the world beneath
the stars and named ourselves:
the Golden Age, the Age to Come
and all across the land we reaped:

our sickles shone and blood flowed red
in endless rivers in the sun.
With bill and hook and steel and fire
we took the wondrous kingdom's gold
and found strange pleasures and stranger
pains wherever we made our beds.
We rambled on the wayward track; now
the warp and weft of life wear thin:
the threads are frayed and all undone:
we cannot return, we cannot stay,
we cannot travel on.

Frail and weary like lonely ghosts
we wait abandoned by the trail,
until we find a voice that calls
among the walls of moss-grown stone
as in the dusk the evening wraiths
chase setting sun and rising moon.
The shadows draw the shadow-paths
by an ancient flint-stone church
and lead us over the greenest grass
to bow our heads before the scythe
and find our rest at last.

All Fires Light the Wicker Man

Scott J. Couturier

All fires light the Wicker Man—
burn higher, higher, as we sing this song!
Morris dancers mark the tune,
praising Sun & praising Moon,
hobby-horse hungry for virginity
as we raise worship to our trinity:
for the Goddess of the Orchards
& the grim God of the Waves,
& last the Summer's searing sun,
day-bright beacon of divinity.

All fires light the Wicker Man—
burn higher, higher, as we sing this song!
Within, a sacrifice writhes & screams,
even as the brass band blares
& mad hares in dozens break the seams
of Winter-cold earth beneath out feet!
The frame goes up in startling flame,
roasting alive our offered game
beside a heathen Christian's life.
Hey, ho, cups full to utmost brim!
All hail coming of May's Queen!

All fires light the Wicker Man—
burn higher, higher, as we sing this song!
The shepherd's servant roasts alive

as we fall to revelry in throng,
mad rutting midst the ash & blood,
clad only in coiling crowns of furze
as Summer's first lust is slaked.
The sun sets as the Wicker Man's head
falls inward with a roaring flood
of flame: the heretic (still alive!)
for a final time wails out Christ's name.

All fires light the Wicker Man—
burn higher, higher, as we sing this song!
Let the harvest be plentiful, & the Summer long!

Zombie Moon

Margaret Curtis

Disease has crept across this blighted land,
Its shadow cast o'er every hearth and home.
We sacrifice to stay Death Angel's hand
While portents of our end are forced to roam
Along familiar streets, now still and bare.
Inside each house we cease, withal, to care,

Unless it is to pray that we be spared,
Or that our end is meaningful, or leads
To something better, something dared—
A truth, an essence, something from past deeds
That proves for this we're wholly unprepared
And on the face of Judgment once we stared.

That visage of Death's Angel passing o'er
Reminds us of some prophecy, arcane,
When tribes were slaves of Pharaohs, kings of Yore,
Tyrannical and cruel lords of pain,
Who used up lives to build their tombs in vain
And squandered Earth's good harvest for their gain.

So how have we become them? How might we,
With great machines that build—now peace, now war—
Refuse this sign for all humanity:
CHANGE NOW OR DIE writ large upon our door?
Is it too late? A Zombie's bite cuts deep
This Full-Moon-tide, and I'm too tired to sleep.

What is that truth, quintessence of the soul?
What sacrifice could we, collective, make?
The sum of all our parts create a whole
That's greater than each single life at stake.
A change of heart now couldn't come too soon
For all of us beneath this Zombie Moon.

Eidolon Tetratych

Frank Coffman

(After Thomas Bailey Aldrich's "Eidolon"—
the four epigraphs are sections of that sonnet.)

I. The Night's Children

Those forms we fancy shadows, those strange lights
That flash on lone morasses, the quick wind
That smites us by the roadside are the Night's
Innumerable children.

Near-hidden in the depths of Night—but darker—
Are the myriad beings from a different *Zone*.
Those uneasy times you feel you are not alone . . .
You are right! Those phantom dim marsh lights grow starker
And flash in brutal brilliance if you fare too close
The sudden frosty breeze that chills your cheek,
Might well be *Something* one should never seek.
Night's Spawn—those shadowy forms know no repose.

Of the vast and countless legion of the ancient dead
A still vast portion linger near our plain.
A huge, horrific number who remain
With powers *to journey back* and hither tread.
Oh yes! They are with us here, our plague and plight.
They are the spectral *Children of the Night*.

II. Unconfined

> *. . . Unconfined*
> *By shroud or coffin, disembodied souls,*
> *Still on probation, steal into the air*
> *From ancient battlefields and churchyard knolls*
> *At the day's ending . . .*

As day and life depart and the lych bell tolls,
And corpse remains, the spirit gone, that knell
Most often means departure for those souls
To wend their ways to Heaven or to Hell.
But there are many—far too many—wights
Who are condemned to linger near us here.
Though many are merely *lost, Some* are to Fear!
And can return to us to haunt our nights.

A soldier slain in a battle long forgotten,
Who himself relished slaying other men.
And others who believed it no great sin
To use their fellows ill—such souls are rotten!
The misbegotten, most amoral brood
Whose thoughts were foul and deeds were never good.

III. The Dusk of Hope

> *. . . Pestilence and despair*
> *Fly with the startled bats at set of sun;*

No, They are not confined in crypt or coffin
These bringers of stark Fear and dire Despair.
Foreboded by foul, pestilential air
When they impinge upon us here—quite often
Miasmatic mists and horrid dim-lit portal
Demark their entry points. You must beware
Their presence—sensed first in the very air!
Sickening, chill, the bane of all who are mortal.

They are the ones for whom all hope has fled,
The foredoomed spirits of the restless dead.
Among fleet flying bats at set of sun
They hover close—and closer till the dawn
But the Night is far their favorite demesne.
Then they roam free. And woe if they are seen!

IV. Sold Souls

And wheresoever murders have been done,
In crowded palaces or lonely woods,
Where'er a soul has sold itself and lost
Its high inheritance, there, hovering, broods
Some mute, invisible, accursèd ghost.

Especially cursed are those who most foully slew
Their fellow creatures by cruel plot or plan:
Whether an assassin of a king or queen,
Or some foul fiend, killing one they never knew
To satisfy a lust for pain and blood,
Or take a life seeking to gain in power.
Their essence is ever condemned to loom and lower—
A curse upon us, Antithesis of Good.

The great inheritance of a soul that might have been
Has been sold or thrown aside by these *Long Lost.*
These and their ilk come back through that Door, once crossed
Was never meant to be journeyed through again.
And so, we must know, who dwell on the Living Side,
Night's Children return through a *Portal* open wide.

Written in Smoke

Ann K. Schwader

The stars are farther now. This burning world
has veiled them from us: constellations fade
from myth to rumor, cautionary tales
untimely silenced in the crisis. Lost
as well, that solitary satellite
we trampled, then abandoned like the trees
we breathe as ashes. This is not our air,
our rising ruined water. Redesigned
for unsuspected overlords from void
as vast as failed imagination, Earth
awaits a future fled from us. As fires
turned pyres send up their clouds of camouflage
against the vanished night, we shall not see
what writhes inside it. Mercy, then, at least.

The Beast with a Billion Stomachs

Maxwell I. Gold

In some crooked ocean place where nightmares gargled, slithering under fungal crevasses, past the known reaches of thought, a chimeric beast with a billion stomachs lurked, awoken from a slumber of shadow and death. Awful pictures painted in dank brackets, ruined palaces, and cavernous troughs littered the crumbled seabed where the flesh of curious men was lured by foul, carrion smells towards a vast, gaping maw.

Flee, they thought. Even the pathetic creatures of the sea knew something truly terrifying, seething with carrion and rot past towering rows of hideous teeth, had risen prepared to swallow an ungrateful world. History recalled the thing a plenty of unthinkable, unholy names.

>   Kraken / Cetus,
>>   Leviathan / Devil.

Soon, the world, bereft and stripped of banal mundanity watched as the skies were charred by ash and gold as it frothed near the surface by acidic oceans, where tidal furies slammed against shiny coastlines while plastic cities tumbled into the yawning teeth of a great, hungry mouth.

Flee, we thought, but too late we were to realize that as the oceans were awoken and prepared to devour the world as a chimeric beast with a billion stomachs was now free from a slumber of shadow and death.

The Whippoorwill

Lori R. Lopez

Upon a tense errand, I trudged crossly through
The sediment and slush of a lugubrious milieu
    Forsaken, downcast, veins coursing cold fire
    And nothing could allay the depths of this mire

I have walked in the night, the most solitary jaunts
Through village or city, long graveyardish haunts
    With moxie aquiver; my courage at stake
    Scarce hope of surviving to greet the daybreak

Yet the present bleak patch had my senses on high
Banshee sirens rang shrilly while drawing nigh
    To the gate of a boneyard swirling with fog
    Shrouding the earth like a snow-mantled bog

Apprehension rendered Night an ink-spilled sheen
More frigid to the touch than a frost-laden scene
    Nerve and heat absorbed by suspenseful silence
    Pressing down above spirits stored in exilence

I shuddered forth at a death-marching pace
As if going to my funeral, which might be the case!
    Could the shades touch my flesh? I hadn't a notion
    My steps ankle-deep in a thick moonlit ocean

Praying to whatever the Universe offered
Robbed of concern for the skeletons coffered
    I tramped sunken plots with haste and abhorrence
    Endeavoring to leave them in states of ignore-ance—

Attention was captured by a mournful wail
Disrupting the calm of souls past the Veil
    What harbinger beckoned ears the dark froze?
    Did the voice seek to halt a heart's decompose?

There in the corner by a crumbling stone wall
On the branch of a ghost tree a bird would enthrall
    With orbs twice the hue of two bottomless holes
    Like beads of Black Onyx, a dim pair of coals

And as Midnight tolled, agitating the gloom
Countless brumes slipped out of a stagnant doom
    Uprooted in the murk by a blood-chilling pall
    The cry of a Whippoorwill—dismal its call

"Please pay some respect by ceasing your chatter!"
I claimed I had come for the urgent-most matter
    Beseeching the creature to lend a kind wing
    And find in its breast the grace not to sing

Instead a large mouth repeated its name—
Over and over it uttered the same . . .
    No Raven or Hoot Owl, no Mocker or Jay
    Just a simple Nightjar shooing phantoms away!

Aloof to my pleas; a blind eye to the sight
When I stumbled to both knees in a serious plight
    "Here lies my dear mother, a saint in her tomb
    I only brought sorrow since leaving the womb."

Praying the bad omen bite its fey tongue
Until I conveyed earnest sentiments wrung
    For a mother to hear the belated apology
    "Bird, if you could, allow a quick elegy!"

I begged the bugbear one small consideration
A scrap of mercy from incessant oration
    Many were the tales of woe and regret—
    Of dancing with Grief like a Death Minuet

In a Whippoorwill's presence the sorriest luck
By the length of its song would fates be struck
    Did the featherbane summon a feast of lost souls
    After waking the buried as hungry as Trolls?

The critter's gaze reflected my own despair
Blinking at jitters with a sympathetic air
    "Years have you scorned us for being a jinx
    Though we are not the onus everyone thinks."

A quiet tone informed she had been misunderstood
Her gift to the world may not symbolize good
    But a cemetery eve was immune to all curse:
    The solitary place she could never make worse!

Digging Beneath the Battlefield

Ypres, Belgium, October 1918

Steven Withrow

I

We dug; we dug for fifteen hours
With picks, pails, hauling ropes, and shovels
To twice the depth of a grave. Ours,
And by this I mean Lieutenant Lovell's
And mine, was a partnership-in-crime.
Finding China, fossils, or oil
Would've taken much less time
Than our invasion of the soil.

In the Allied Army, we'd got word
From a Belgian of a Dark One at Ypres:
A buried Worm-Chimera scored
In serpent scales and boils. The Sleeper,
Interrupted, had scorched Earth before.
We leaned to our shovels, began to dig more.

II

The chamber, when we struck its top,
Resounded like a ship's hull. We
Shuddered but didn't think to stop;
We'd brought the tools to set it free:
A welding torch, some light explosives,
A spell to lift the more arcane
Defenses. The air stank of corrosives
In the pit we'd dug. A drenching rain
Made puddles, and though it was ten days
After the battle, the mud looked red
With blood of men, or the Dark One's ichor.
We soothed our shell-shocked nerves with liquor,
Renewed our vow to join the dead
When we gave the Beast the Earth to raze.

[Note: A copy of this poem, in scrawled ink, was discovered among a war-addled private's belongings in a wing of Craiglockhart Hospital in Edinburgh at the end of 1918. The author, who died of the grippe, was from Stoke-on-Trent. There is no record of a "Lieutenant Lovell" in his battalion. An incomplete third part began simply, "We've opened Hell—such soulless eyes!" before trailing off into incoherency.]

The Dark Sorcerer

Charles Lovecraft

The sorcerer delivered his black song,
And people fell down in the streets on fire.
Even as he raised his chant, as of cracked gong,
The flaming shrieks of local folk grew higher.
Thick swamps of croaking frogs now raised their throng
Of answering calls to his funeste desire,
To catch and gulp down souls who had died *wrong*,
And great frogs were that never seemed to tire.

Twisted and malformed, the evil one retired
And wondered why the world so often wronged,
That people such as he, long Satan-sired,
Should get away with vileness such as thronged
Within his breast that blackened mind had fired?
He shrugged, and went back to the frogs and longed.

On Finding the Man

Holly Day

the dog finds the man first, sniffs confused
at the pool of blood by his hand. in its mythology
this man is always upright, noisy, exuding clouds of purple tobacco
    smoke
never still and quiet. the death of this man
does not fit into the dog's cosmology
is a crushing blow to its faith.

later, birds find the man, tiny sparrows
drawn to the clouds of nits and flies
already building great fortresses in his blood-caked hair
claiming him for various
insect kingdoms. crows settle, chase sparrows away
flick aside the audacious flies, their arraying, wiggling young
dig past the layer of dried flesh and blood
find rapture in fresh meat.

As the Dream Descends

Kurt Newton

As the dream descends, my body deflates,
chest and torso sink into the mattress;
I slip down into the Underland,
where unnamed creatures lie in wait,
their faces white and featureless,
in chambers cold and damp.

What follows next is always the same,
I navigate the catacombs in fear that death
will extend its cold, white hand
and stop me before I can escape.
But then the morning sun fills my head,
and I rise a free and thankful man.

I once believed that dreams were safe,
playgrounds of imaginative excess
that ease the mind of the day's demands.
But what follows me when I wake,
is a feeling of unspeakable duress,
as if pursued by something damned.

This horror is due to the pact I made,
a youthful indiscretion I must confess,
with forces I did not fully understand:
my theoretical soul in exchange

for a life of supreme success;
the outcome of which I surely did not plan.

Imagine my surprise when every day
good fortune rained at my behest,
and soon I was richer than the richest man.
I knew then the debt I'd have to pay
would be my soul and nothing less,
and so the dreams began.

And here I am, as once again I brace
for the inevitable nightly harness
that lowers me amid those who hold command.
For I know if I should lose my way,
the sun won't rise and I'll be left bereft,
another unnamed creature of the Underland.

The Poltergeists of Park Slope

LindaAnn LoSchiavo

The memory knocks insistently, rattles its chain. The story retold,
summoned, shared like leftovers from a phantom feast. My uncle's voice,
an incantation that wiped the table clean of holiday food, poured the
chill down the backs of our collars, goosefleshed our arms, explaining
how most ghosts are a disappearing act whereas poltergeists engineer
noisy return engagements. Voids of vaudeville, greedy for a live audience.

A lifetime ago, his weekly poker game was dinner-theatre for restless
spirits stuck in a haunted house. Now those long-ago scares rose like
steam, as a flayed turkey breast releases its heat to the carving knife,
while his words basted our imagination. Not the rapping, tapping Poe
heard on his chamber door but came the crashing, smashing of crockery
shelved in invisible china cabinets, glassware thrown at the stove, forcing
the players to their feet. Only to find nothing.

Or the evenings when spooks overturned the table, sending hearts
and clubs airborne, alarming all. Mouthfuls of memories gnawed at the
apparition's loneliness, letting it be regurgitated, coating the kitchen
with chaos.

Priests came and went, their blessings, novenas, incense, prayers
brittle as glass. Nothing lived in these invocations: no exorcism, no
catharsis.

Collectively, our blood forgets the promise of surge and flow as we
shiver on the brink of the climax. My uncle's closing act, ventriloquy,
fills the room with unhinged cackling, a poltergeist maniacally gleeful.
Proud of its performance as our soup pot boils dry and our percolator
shrieks.

Years after, I ponder. In dreams I envision what my uncle (a teenager then) could not: a slow-cooked rage, the soughing wind taunting pulled-down shades, tattered scullery wallpaper scuffed by body slams. A furious spouse. Abuse accumulated, stoking a fire in the belly. Well-oiled revenge readying, seething, sharpening a six-inch boning knife. A marital ragout charred, redness splattering. Now a dirge lullabies her ears as she swoons for a shovel, lozenges the word *burial* under her tongue. At last there's a sense of the future humming. Except strange chortling is suddenly unlocked.

The empty jar of morning will be filled with a doorful of white coats, a restraining garment nearly split open by wild whoops of merriment. Emotions drowned in this kitchen will resurface, be resuscitated. Have the last laugh.

City of Carrion, Valley of Darkness

Harris Coverley

Across the vast swathes of ether, through the cold indifference of the space between desolate stars, lies a hidden and forgotten world, a world of cool dirt desert, sealed in twilight, and cracked in gigantic valleys across its surface by a sun that has long since lost its vigour. In the middle of its surface, deep within one of those cracks, there is a river of dark water, and on an island in the middle of the river dwells a city of the forbidden.

The city is fair enough for most of the year, its peoples going about their livelihoods with love and joy and sadness and pain as much as in any other place, and all is sound . . . until the bodies float up. From some even deeper realm below the crust they come: huge, ugly, twisted, already half-decayed, the forms of colossal men, and yet *not-men*, but abhuman beasts unworthy of a name, that must in our reality stalk the ruminations of diseased minds. Every year they rise, and the city is stricken with a festival of despicable delirium.

As the bodies land on the island's craggy beaches, the fishermen howl out, and the rest of the city joins them, stopping their work, stripping off their clothes, running to the shores with knives and swords and clubs and pitchforks. They slit the carrion flesh open and paint their skin with clotted blood, a thousand shades of red in arabesque designs, before tearing off what they can, fighting each other for what they believe to be the best cuts, and eating their servings raw. When but bones remain they split them open and suck them dry, before beginning to dance, all of the city's populace, dancing and dancing, with each other and in selfish fits, before they fall to the floor and vomit up their rotted portions . . . and the day after all returns to normal, until the next rising . . .

Up until last night I visited this evil place in dreams only as a ghost, unnoticed by the citizenry, moving on the winds of that valley of darkness. But then, in a terrible sleep, I found my own body washed up upon the city's shore, my blood painted on those hysteric skins, had my flesh torn, consumed by vicious teeth, and was thrown up in the streets. Every last cut, every last chewing, every lash of the tongue, every drip of retching . . . every feeling but finality. And now I dread slumber like one dreads the coming of death, when I might just return to that city as a meal, or possibly worse . . .

Hand of Glory

Manuel Arenas

The hanged man's hand, perched on a stand, glows weirdly in the night,
Its waxen fingers bearing wicks that burn an eldritch light.
When held aloft, it opens locks without the need for keys,
Leaving occupants motionless to do with as you please.
Pluck the moldering gibbet fruit: the dead man's reddened hand.
Swaddle in an ebon mortcloth, black as a mourning band.
Pickle it in piss, herbs, and salt, a fortnight then ferment.
Parch the paw in the dog-day sun, to bake in malintent.
Render the carcass in a vat into dead man's tallow,
Then slather the ghastly trophy, to seal and unhallow
Wicks plucked from out the crow-pecked head.
Where'er it shines its baleful light, so darkness too shall shed.

In a Haunted Holler

Adam Bolivar

In a haunted holler   under hills of blue
Bides jumping Jack   the Giant-Killer,
Hopping like a hare   hither and yon,
Sneaky and sly   with a sundry bag of tricks.
Ghosts and goblins   give him no trouble,
And all in those parts   ask him for help
When the hounds of hell   howl in the night,
When Old Scratch springs out   of the sunken mire
Searching for souls   to snatch in his claws.
Jack deals the Devil   a damning blow,
Twisting his traps   and turning them around,
Sending Scratch   scurrying into the earth.
In Hell unwelcome,   from Heaven cast out,
Jack wanders the wood,   a wild man in rags,
His lantern's light   lingering on,
In a haunted holler   under hills of blue.

Lines on the Mistress of an Old Sea-Town

Manuel Pérez-Campos

This young mermaid in chaplet and arrested
gracility of motion was conceived in stone
for an islet in an annular basin.
She is combing out kelp from her long hair
and looking sideways at how the day has fled.
She is the hub for every wanderer
who has lost his ability for prayer,
for the stark readiness of her twist-prone
fluke is a reminder of how easy
it is to banish from self-consciousness
the tyranny of unfaith, simply by
refusing to be engaged for a spell
by all that landlocks one, just as she is:
for if she were to truly sense us, she
would vanish like noon-struck ice, in a sizzle.

Those That We Meet in Dark Country Lanes

Darrell Schweitzer

Those that we meet in dark country lanes,
should not be mistaken for the little people,
for they are not always little,
or necessarily people.
They leave strange footprints:
Was that a fox, or a goat,
or even a small horse?
Or one of them?
They converse in barks, chirps, and whistles,
though, being neither fallen nor unfallen,
they know the speech of angels.
With music and liquors they make us mad,
and lead us into the deep woods,
until, laughing and singing and deliriously afraid,
we come to the place where the earth opens up,
and the ancient rites begin.

The God of Dark Fantasy Prose-Poetry

Jay Sturner

In fall I bloom from waning light, inhale the air of brightly dying leaves. In winter I stretch across iron skies and bathe in blue starlight. Come spring I'll fragment into a million tired blackbirds and merge with summer storms. Always, it seems, my energies wax and wane. For hours, days, weeks at a time, I may meet not a soul. But whatever the hour, whatever the season, I keep to routine: stroll the lanes, admire the moon, wait for summoning. And when called upon, gloom and beauty uncoil at my feet like young dragons.

I came into proper existence during an autumnal equinox. Oh, I remember it well! I'd found myself within a soft pool of candlelight on an old writing desk, brought forth by a man whose dark eyes beamed decadent dreams; the man called Baudelaire. All that night we wrote, our energies intertwined in a spectral dance, wherein I sewed beastly wings to the black, faceless worms of his subconscious mind—ideas he promptly snatched from their chittering flight and imprisoned in prose-poems.

Before that night, I was an aimlessly wandering particle of dream, a moth deep in the caverns of Man's collective unconscious. An embryonic muse, if I may—little known, and rarely summoned. But *that* was the night, the collaboration, which propelled me out of my nebulous aspect! After which, in watery reflections and moonlit windows, I began to see, though faintly, the azure eyes and coal black wings of my true form. How the poet did this I do not know—the power of the genius mind may be, in and of itself, a creator of gods and demons.

And divine I became! Made a deity, as it were, of dark prose-poetry; borne through the haunted portal of Baudelaire. I think now of those we influenced—Rimbaud, Smith, Pugmire, etc.—who conjured my spirit and channeled my energies into the content of their ever-fantastical compositions. Who forged for me a static identity and furthered my status as a muse-god. Who, by presenting our collaborations to the world, led me to the throne of my current incarnation: the God of Dark Fantasy Prose-Poetry.

Aubade

Paul Grant

He had awoken willing it gone, but it had clung to his consciousness like
some filthy parasite. We are inclined to be impatient with nightmares,
but when they *impinge* in this way, when they *interfere* with daylight—what
damage they cause! Cool water was never so welcome. Even the coarse
feel of the towel was a blessing. Any and every sign of reality, all
reminders that the dream was just *that* and nothing more. And then the
clearest sign, the surest proof: her familiar step on the stair. Such
comfort, such relief in that simple sound! As she came into the bedroom
he turned with a smile to greet her, then recoiled. She had no face.
Wailing, he backed into the corner, waving his arms before him. His
nightmare stood, composed; then slowly, and very deliberately,
advanced.

Starfall

Melissa Ridley Elmes

I sat at the window of my bedroom, idly gazing
into the darkness descending,
watching the last light of day fold itself
into the horizon, tucked into the warm mantle
of night. Into the blue-black space, I saw
fireflies make their appearance,
darting hither and thither without pattern or trajectory,
blinking into view, then cloaking themselves
in darkness again. Presently, the sky opened,
dripping wee lights, and I looked closer to see
these falling drops were not fireflies, but the very stars,
raining down like a gentle spring drizzle—why?
I cannot say. I fell asleep to the sound of starfall,
waking to a starless sky and burn marks on the pavement,
a firefly asleep on my nose, its dark bottom
lighting up anew with each tiny snore.

The Mimics

Christina Sng

One hundred days

And still, I am frozen
In flashbacks, dying
Over and over again
As I write this testament:

There are monsters wearing
Human skin that walk the Earth:
Empty, hollowed-out shells, insides
Long devoured by hungry gods.

But they know things—
Weapons they use to maim us,
Cripple us so we do their bidding
As they leech away our life force,

They mimic us, all the things
That make us good and true
To fill the gaping hole where a life,
A love, a conscience should be.

Tests show them as normal,
The ones who get caught.
People with normal minds
Masking the horrific truth.

I have long fled from them,
But fear still clutches me
Like a child clasped around
Her mother's ankle,

Screaming for her
To stop before she steps
Into the trap laid there
By the monsters.

Fear is my safety net,
My warning beacon.
Fear saved my life
When I listened.

Now I need to regrow
All that I have lost.
Or grow new parts—
Parts with thorns,

Parts that hurl stones
And slay monsters.
Parts that protect me,
Not destroy me.

I will grow
A thickened armor,
Learn to identify
And battle monsters.

I will train my children
To be strong, to channel
Their fear into a rage,
A radar, a protective power.

We will hunt them all down
And hurl them out of Earth
Into the desolation of space,
Leaving them alone and adrift

Where they can look into
The mirror of their cold,
Soulless hearts and know
That is where they belong.

Gilgamesh in Mourning

Geoffrey Reiter

How is it, then, that we—the men who fought
The monster of the shadowed woods in battle,
Who spilled his brackish blood in dirt, who caught
Capricious Ishtar's bull, the cosmic cattle,
And broke its vaulted night-bright horns to hang
Within our Uruk halls—should be now laid
So low? Enkidu, dearest friend, who sang
Attending by my side now lies outsplayed,
A cold and waxen corpse. The fiery queen
Of heaven flaming in galactic lust
To burn my dead friend's festered flesh, gangrene
And worms to gore him to the House of Dust.
If this is life's end, 'neath the writhing scythe,
I cry to vacant sky, "I fear this death!"

The King in Yellow
(A Series of Sijo)

Ngo Binh Anh Khoa

The pages show the fabled play that dooms the ones who read its lines,
Among whom, me— allured by lust for knowledge dark, to my regret.
I have seen His cursed Yellow Sign and trod Carcosa's gloomy streets.

Upon His throne, the deity reigns—the towering King in Yellow draped,
As fearsome as a cancerous Sun that sears deep fear unto one's soul.
On my knees, I don't dare to breathe nor view His mask—which,
bulging, shifts.

What eldritch sights beneath those robes, I neither know nor wish to see;
Caught in His gaze, I can do naught except bow low and mutely pray.
All in vain. Here, there's but one god to hear my prayers and cruelly laugh.

Author's Note: A sijo is a traditional Korean poetic form that consists of
three lines with 14 to 16 syllables per line on average. However, a
modern sijo may not strictly follow the aforementioned rules, especially
the ones written in English. Hence, a modern sijo is more flexible, and
the number of syllables in each group within a line may change
depending on each writer. The most interesting part of a sijo is in the
final line, which starts with a "twist." This "twist" traditionally consists of
the first three syllables of the line (followed by the subsequent five
syllables), presenting a change in the meaning, sound, or poetic device
that makes the whole line stands out, leading to the conclusion.

The Dominion of the Son of the Dragon

Jordan Zuniga

In the darkness of the night,
Where the shadows were to dwell,
In the coldest part of the north,
Where the ice would surely swell,

In the twisting of the caverns,
Where earth is deep below,
In the places mortals do not tread,
Where few could surely know,

In the midst of ancient evil,
Where they sat as the master's tool,
In the plotting and the scheming,
Where none would challenge their liege's rule,

In the darkness of the north,
Where none would play the fool,
In the darkness of the north,
The realm, of King Dracul . . .

City of Dreams

Maxwell I. Gold

I dream in cities, ancient towers, and metal bones where nothing made sense. Roads without direction and traffic lights shaped like conch shells swirled underneath a blood-sky all smelled of rust and death. I tried to find my way out, traveling past some rotted conservatory riddled with dead greenwood, purple stinkhorn, and bloated fungi. In the distance I saw the muted skyline of my home, decayed and ruinous as I drove onward to a place as the world behind fell into a river of muck and sewage. I felt my surroundings suddenly explode with a toxic salaciousness, cluttered and heavy, trumped by those enigmatic bodies.

They clouded my sight and reason, changing the roads and twisting the horizon overhead as bony girders wrenched across my ears in some awful tubular dance. Somehow, all at once, I stood at the same boulevard where I began under that strange Fibonaccian shell as if I were wandering down a path towards my own oblivion with mathematical precision. Streetlamps and wires dangled overhead while the gaunt structures swayed in the blood-sky, ominous and cruel, leaving me to gaze o'er the horizon of my home. Rebuilding and destroying itself through an infinite process, only then did I understand that I dream in cities, confined to the mass and mayhem of galactic cellars composed of steel, gold, and concrete without direction, where nothing made sense.

The Outsider

Carl E. Reed

> We are imprisoned in life in the company of persons
> powerfully unlike us.
>
> —Ralph Waldo Emerson

I reject your pallid myths & sickly hymns
fashioned to extoll the most perverse
laughable humancentric good acts & sins
of zero weight or worth to universe.
I ripple through green forests with fleet deer,
chant before black altars of my kind,
sway to ethereal music of the spheres,
sing paeons to gods pagan & sublime.
Nietzschean: my sorrow & my mirth—
I reject the Apollonian, fairy-kissed.
Switched with puling infant after birth—
the Dionysiac outsider in your midst.
Ever have I caused you grief & pain:
trickster changeling of scheming elvish skein.

Zwartenberg the Necromancer

Manuel Arenas

For eight nights Ba'al Zwartenberg trafficked amongst the gravestones in the mission boneyard, swathed in the tattered cerements of a Papago man who had been interred in a secluded cairn off-site, but not far enough it seems to have escaped the purview of the sorcerer and his infernal informants. Once discovered, his harried minion, Diego, dug up the grave, whereupon the warlock leapt into the open cavity and snuggled up to the brittle bones with the familiarity of a lover, after which he took on the habiliments of the ancient cadaver as his own. Now the fearful yet faithful servant would serve the new master of the Burning Ember Mission from his violated grave in the tawny Helldorado brush.

On some nights, the warlock would prowl the Helldorado Necropolis and break into the mausoleums of the town elite to take trophies and desecrate their dreamless sleep in a most profane and ungodly manner. On the ninth night, Ba'al Zwartenberg repaired to the mission mortuary chapel with his man Diego to prepare for a Cimmerian ritual: the grim and unholy rite of raising the dead.

The blood-orange moon hung heavy and low like an overripe fruit, fit to burst over the shadow-laden rooftops of the Helldorado eventide. Distant telephone lines and sparse tree branches loomed faintly in the foreground leaving marly streaks across the ocherous orb, occluding the path of its amber beams. The vesper bell of the Burning Ember Mission clanged, disturbing the resident bats that had taken up in the belfry causing them to decamp as dirgelike chants issued from within its spectral halls, carried on rank breezes insinuating their sinister strands into the windows of the neighboring homes and into the ears of their quiescent denizens, whispering words of doom and despair to inform their nightmares.

Marching in solemn procession, the Master, clad in the cerements of the grave, and fingering the fell charms on his grisly choker, declaims an insalubrious panegyric, prevailing over the intermittent bleats of a black goat kid that he bears in his arms. At his heels, his ebon-robed acolyte holds aloft a ponderous tome: the dreaded *Cultes des Goules,* of the Comte d'Erlette. The duo filed into the mission burial vault wherein awaited an altar draped in a black mantel, surmounted by the accoutrements of Thanatotic ritual, dimly illumined by inky candles. The atmosphere, redolent with the stench of charnel spoils, is compounded by the burning patchouli emanating from a nearby thurible. In the center of the tomb is a salt-rimmed circle containing a vitreous casket wherein lies a mummied corpse in sepulchral quietude. About its neck is a jade amulet carven into the likeness of a hound from Hell. The acolyte took up the chant as the supplicant opened the door to the casket, exposing, in all its desiccated splendor, the ghastly occupant therein.

Taking pains not to smudge the circle, he stepped away from the casket then, leveling an obsidian athame to the throat of his bleating sacrifice, drew the blade across its throat, releasing a crimson font that he directed toward a chalice within the circle before stepping back. A murky effluvium soon expelled from the maw of the mummy, wending its way to the chalice, which it temporarily engulfed. Swirling atop the brim of the chalice, the tiny whirlwind counter-siphoned the contents of the chalice up a pitchy track into the shriveled mouth of the brittle sallow corpse, which fleshed out with the sanguinary sustenance. Then, with a stertorous gasp and a croak, the revivified revenant shot open its reconstituted eyes and stirred to rise from its narrow house.

Our Last Halloween

Adele Gardner

For our last Halloween
we wore cat masks,
thin cardboard cut
from a catfood giveaway
tied on with string.
Your sad dark eyes
looked out at me, mismatched
through kid-size holes.
Maybe your cold kept you subdued.
You baked small Halloween drop cookies
the size of silver dollars or Easter money
with chocolate black cats in the middle.
Our cats chased Halloween toys:
a mini-pumpkin, Frankenstein's hairy eyeball,
little catnip puffs of ghosts and werewolves
they greedily snapped up
and carried in their mouths, protecting us
from evil—including ourselves.
No fights that night as we watched Garfield,
fielded five cats, toasted each other
with witches' brews, ate pumpkin-painted donuts,
and gave each other Halloween treats:
a cloth basket like a black cat's head,
marshmallow ghosts, a puppet raven,
your favorite peanut butter sweets in orange wrappings,

but best of all
the tussle-rumbling and scary-loud purrs
of big boy catnipped cats
pouncing on the goblins
tethered at the ends of our strings.

Crypt Currency

Wade German

'Neath muslin covers
    Sighs a spell:
A phantom hovers
    Nigh, to tell
Truth to lovers
    Bound for Hell,
Each blind before black gate,
      Laughing late:

"O souls whose scheming
    Sped to gold,
Thine corpses teeming
    Vermin hold;
Dimly dreaming,
    Enter mould.
The prince and fool each pay,
      Same the way.

"As worms keep wisdom
    Down the grave,
To throne in thraldom
    Bow, and pave
Them their kingdom's
    Writhing wave:
Such soil thine souls shall turn,
      Richly earn!"

—*After Beddoes*

The Pixie-Ring

Scott J. Couturier

Ring of mushrooms by the wayside—
what within your fey perimeter abides?
A shiver of silvern bells at dusk
sounds as evening exhales its musk:
orbs on the dark garth swarm & glide.

Ring of mushrooms, mottled red in hue—
who tempts your periphery will Faery rue.
Perilous Realm lures down uncanny trails,
seducing hapless hikers beyond the veil
of tableaux which mortal ken must eschew.

Above, sere oak leaves of umber cast
rattle like rotted teeth, fair Summer past.
Fungi flourish in hoary dales of gloom,
pale caps clammy with November's doom—
the pixie-ring is wilted, with blight aghast.

Perish back to the pitch-black loaming,
gateway sealed by Autumn's gloaming!
Elfin songs grow strained as first snow falls,
retreating to fabulous jewel-fret halls
where the enrapt revel, faery-ales foaming.

Serenade for Black Plague Gwynneth

Manuel Pérez-Campos

Slight form still giddy with vanity, albeit with festering boils
on forearms and treacly countenance, curtsy to me in your tattered
damask and conical hat: although I be a skeleton in a scarlet
cloak, accept my spindly hand and shirk not from my spectral
tone: I love your wanness, your weakness, the wantonness
of your malaise: those wild, novice gestures of unvoiced despair

at a handheld mirror which foreshadow how your flesh will
continue to decay to further suit my taste as you accept
the flattery of my rejoicing in the way you arrive at me, the young,
ill-met poacher in homespun patchwork garb shoulder-touched
whilst flaying a deer as though by an Archangel gathering
those who are doomed on the Day of Wrath and at whose pledge

of devotion you refused to smile: there is moonlight on your forehead
now as you sleep, like a portal into your dreams: let us saraband
to imaginary music out here in this intimate grove of browned
woodbine, near the castle of your ancestors, from which you have
been cruelly expelled, and we shall pause as needed, aloof to
the charm of goldfinch and rose, that you may cough out more

of the hell which resides behind your botched teeth: listen, your true love, the fine greyhound trained to follow you, is howling as though worms were at work already, tailoring you to be fit to reign with me: be not alarmed, like me you will never not be free: when you are found by servants and banished at last with spade and swinging censer he, to allay the horror of his solitude, will disinter you.

The Lorelei

A German Legend

Frank Coffman

A huge and jagged cliff of dark grim slate
Rises above the Rhine, cutting the sky.
And sailing men have found their place to die
Beneath that "Murmuring Rock," meeting their fate.
For *She* croons there atop that craggy height
And, with her singing, lures them to the rocks
With silver sibilant song and golden flowing locks—
Breaking ships . . . and the silence of the night.

The Lorelei lurks there and weaves a message
To all unwary sailors who dare that passage.
Who know the legend pray the Saints deliver
Them from her beck and call, from that dire shore.
Still many are enthralled, steer toward Death's Door,
And meet the rocks and doom beneath the river.

Classic Reprints

Beside the Dead

Ina Coolbrith

It must be sweet, O thou, my dead, to lie
With hands that folded are from every task;
Sealed with the seal of the great mystery—
The lips that nothing answer, nothing ask.
The life-long struggle ended; ended quite
The weariness of patience, and of pain;
And the eyes closed to open not again
On desolate dawn or dreariness of night.
It must be sweet to slumber and forget;
To have the poor tired heart so still at last:
Done with all yearning, done with all regret,
Doubt, fear, hope, sorrow, all forever past:
Past all the hours, or slow of wing or fleet—
It must be sweet, it must be very sweet!

[From Coolbrith's *A Perfect Day and Other Poems* (San Francisco, 1881).]

The Pearl

Henry Anderson Lafler

In the water pale and clear—
Wan, clear water of the sea—
Laving lands the sun is near
Whither soft and ceaselessly
From the spicy islands—blow—
From the fragrant forests—go
Little winds to charm the sea,
Drifting perfumes to the bay
Where the red-sailed pearl-boats lay—
In a year remote and far,
On a gold and purple day,
When the iris-armored gar,
Breaking water in his play,
Glittered like a silver bar,
And the long, white, curving strand
Hitherside the sweet, green land
Was an ivory scimitar
On a cloak from Samarcand—
Purple with a green-gold band—
Bare brown divers found for me
(In the caverns of the sea—
In the water pale and clear—
Wan, clear water of the sea)
A great pearl and mystery.
I can well remember yet

How with shining bodies wet
They came slow and reverently
Bearing that great pearl to me.

They had found it where a wall
Cold and coral is and tall
Round whose gleaming parapet
Monstrous surges foam and fret,
And whose glimmering base is set
In a vast and dim sea-hall—
In a twilight violet—
In a sepulcher of ships—
On the flowerless ocean-floor,
Stiller than dead girl's lips.

Night by night beneath the moon—
Night by night beneath the stars—
Listening the water's croon
Round the tropic river-bars,
My sad pearl I gazed upon—
Beautiful it was and wan—
All the sweet, warm nights it shone;

And from out its hidden heart
Faintest music seemed to start,

And sad, ghostly murmurings
Of strange sea-enchanted things
Dwelling in dim halls apart;

Murmurings of the galleon
Plunged to shadow from the sun,
And the dreams that drowned men dream
In their sleep but just begun—
Whispers of the brown seaweed
That the untilled levels breed,
Ever swaying in the stream
Like a dancer in a dream;
And the ships that, captainless,
Moored where with black marble mix
Porphyry and sardonyx,
Rot in deep forgetfulness;
And all delicate fair things
Such as some dim-dreaming pool
Hidden from sea-murmurings—
Round and clear and still and cool hollow beautiful—
Marred not save with shadowings
Of the gulls' wide-spreading wings—
Stirred not save when, least of life,
Frail sea-things, ephemeral
In their dim and secret strife

Make a grain of sand to fall,
Opal-colored, fine and small.

Whiter than the whitest star—
Brighter in the bright moonlight
Than a girl's white eyelids are,
Kissed by lover in the night,
Was my pearl unto my sight,
Whispering ever unto me
The eternal mystery
Of the blue, unsceptered sea.

Lost forever is the pearl,
Staked and lost in high carouse
Where the naked dancers whirl
In the hell-hot gaming house;
And they bore over-sea,
And they bore it over-land
For a great queen's treasury—
For a warm white woman's hand—
Far, oh, far, from where the strand,
White as women's souls may be,
Takes beneath the fading moon
Cool caresses of the sea.

*   *   *

And its heart remembers not—
Well I know it hath forgot—
Where the flaring tapers shine
'Mid the fumes of yellow wine
And where clouded-warm it rests
'Twixt a woman's bared breasts—
All forgot, that pearl of mine,
The cool silence under sea,
Wonder, dream, and mystery
Whereof long it whispered me.
whispered me.
Nay, it murmurs now or more
How upon the coral floor
Of the still, empurpled bay
Dimmest, bluest shadows sped
Of the galleys overhead—
Of the silver fish that fled,
Of the golden fish that lay
Quiet all the azure day.

Lost forever is the pearl—
Staked and lost one wild night
Where the painted dancers whirl
In a seeming mad delight.
I shall see it nevermore
Or its glory gaze upon

114

In the moonlight warm and wan
Of the island's scented night;
But a memory I keep,
Dear as dreams and soft as sleep,
Of its magic murmurings
Of the sea's most secret things,
Sweet and holy, treasured deep.

Sad are mine the silver dreams
As walk in ways apart,
And the crystal memory
Of lost and silent heart—
Heart that knew the golden gleams
And the blueness of the streams
And the mystic word, meseems,
Lips of loveliness impart.

Tremulous and silver clear,
Where the warm, soft sea-wind blew,
Listening, my heart did hear
All things marvelous and dear,
Magical and sweet. I knew,
There, the white sea-marge beside,
All its soul, before it died.

[First published in *Sunset* 21, No. 10 (November 1908): 590–93.]

Reviews

Born under Saturn Indeed

Donald Sidney-Fryer

SAMUEL LOVEMAN AND CLARK ASHTON SMITH. *Born under Saturn: The Letters of Samuel Loveman and Clark Ashton Smith.* Edited by S. T. Joshi and David E. Schultz. New York: Hippocampus Press, 2021. 392 pp. $30.00 tpb.

Our review copy of the hefty *Born under Saturn* came to hand on Tuesday afternoon, 31 August 2021. We went to work reading and assimilating it at once. It proved more of a challenge than anticipated, requiring much checking and cross-checking to note most of the inner connections. The overall reading and close examination took us from 31 August to 9 September, no shame or blame on the valorous editors. They have laid out the book with the usual notes, appendix, bibliography, and index, and with their usual editorial care. Bravissimo to them, and all those involved in the project, including the valiant researchers!

Turning to the actual epistles turned into a minor shock, no less than a major revelation. We know Ashton Smith's poetic oeuvre fairly well, but Loveman's much less so. But everything by him that we have conned has borne out what others have opined. Both Smith and Loveman specialized in what is termed "pure poetry"—yes, Pure Poetry—less entangled with or tied to the contemporary world. However, their then personal world was nonetheless closely attached to their own contemporary spheres, cultural and literary. Their close correspondence began through George Sterling in 1913, and then more or less ended soon after Sterling's accidental death in November. We do not consider it a suicide.

He left no note, and he had asked editor B. Virginia Lee to see the proofs of his own column in the *Overland Monthly,* as well as Donald A. Wandrei's notable essay-critique of the four volumes of Smith's poetry, "The Emperor of Dreams," in the issue for December 1926. Smith also affirms that his poet-friend had suffered no noticeable decline in his vital interests and enthusiasms, at least as reported to and by the younger poet.

Of the two poets (both great admirers of Sterling and his multifarious writings) Loveman seems the better adjusted, especially when he went into military service, and then later as a wage-slave. The military refused to induct Smith due to his poor physical condition (an understatement), including obvious underweight, incipient tuberculosis, and general nervousness and irritability (again an understatement). He seemed hardly more than skin and bones. Both poets suffered from what we can term ennui (boredom), discontent, distemper, ill humor, or whatever. Both seem disgruntled, dyspeptic, or neurasthenic.

But when Smith's few but vital needs appeared threatened, he could rise to the occasion. When Prohibition went into effect for more than a decade, Smith responded by making his own bootleg liquor, creating a diversity of wines, whether light or heavy, and thus avoiding the real bootleg, often rotgut. Quite a few people died of the latter, went blind, became paralyzed, etc. If one made their own liquor, and shared it with friends, one could not sell it. One did not advertise at large that one was making their own booze.

Prohibition turned into a costly and medically expensive failure. One might just as well prohibit people from making love! *That* would not work at all! The major apocalypse (strictly speaking, revelation) for us is how Smith not only was divided against his own period, but even against himself. Add to this his natural atrabilia or melancholy, and one has a very disagreeable and unhappy friend or companion. This side of him he kept to himself.

We might surmise, given that Loveman and Smith were both composing some superb poetry, long and short, that they might have found themselves overjoyed. But no! They praised each other's poetry but not that of their own. It is, it would seem, very difficult to be a poetic genius: no happy medium, above all for Smith. Despite his four volumes of poetry, of magnificent stuff, by 1925, and Loveman's poetic rhapsody *The Hermaphrodite* and his play *The Sphinx*, neither bard seemed content or self-satisfied. Like Poe and Baudelaire, they harbored much disdain and resentment toward ordinary people, their contemporary society, however unfair that might seem. They do seem to take pleasure in little things and the occasional romance.

We must state straightforwardly that, although we are quite sympathetic or empathetic to their general emotional plight, it is difficult to feel that way all the time toward either Smith or Loveman while reading these letters, particularly when they seem to be acting against their own self-interest. Smith appears at times to be hilarious, even if unintentionally so. But these are private letters between two friends, even though they would never have wanted to have them published. Heaven forbid!

The volume holds many surprises, no less than signal details, that jump out at one, stirring our poignant sympathy or pointed humor. Here follows a small sampling.

Sam astutely observes to Clark about the latter's unhappy situation that "Too much self-brooding isn't good and writing is always an outlet for such a mood." Sam himself nourishes a half-hearted idea of moving to another city ere long—"And live my life in my own way" (letter 90).

On one occasion when dealing with translations from the French, Clark states correctly that "French verse, as a rule, seems frightfully banal in a word-for-word translation" (letter 91). All too true!

Clark on occasion has minor imaginative notions about the little things that haunt him "with something akin to nostalgia—a homesickness of the unseen and the unknown" (letter 117). He forthwith celebrates the sentiment in the prose-poem "Nostalgia of the Unknown."

The book has only a few pictures. Among them a rare portrait by A. M. Bremer (1915) reveals the young adult Smith at thirty-two (p. 129). He appears both sensitive and quite handsome. Another rare illustration manifests by none other than the poet himself on p. 139, a piece of fantastic art, a weird entity.

Both Clark and Sam cherish the same rare book of prose-poems, *Pastels in Prose*, "which you [Sam] mention reading and [which I] consider one of the treasures of my library." He continues by stating that Stuart Merrill, the translator, has a lofty reputation as a writer of French poetry (letter 145).

Over and over again our pair of poets proclaim their preference for writers like Joseph Conrad and Lafcadio Hearn, not just the powerful novels and other fiction by the former but the latter's exquisite fabrications like *Kwaidan*, *Some Chinese Ghosts*, *Chita*, and *Youma*. Over time succeeding critics and others have confirmed our pair's high opinion of both writers. Their preference for exotic, then little known poetry, like Persian, Chinese, Japanese, etc. is demonstrated time after time throughout their long and intense exchange of letters. Loveman again and again provided Smith with rare but not then necessarily expensive books, at least not during 1913 through 1926.

Just as *The Hashish-Eater* looms large in Smith's output, so too does *The Hermaphrodite* together with the play *The Sphinx* take a commanding position in Loveman's oeuvre. These works also demonstrate over and over and over again that writing as literary creation is in fact genuinely hard work. In a physical sense it is as hard as digging a ditch or chopping wood or making dinner for two dozen people. Never underestimate that labor or travail!

Nor did our pair achieve the three opuses mentioned above, or similar works, in a single day. They sometimes took years to complete and polish. Smith created *The Hashish-Eater* relatively quickly, and at white heat. It took him from 14 January 1920 to or through 13 March, and then further time, to revise and polish where needed. "Rome was not built in a day," nor were these especial masterpieces.

This great body of correspondence between Loveman and Smith— regular heavy-duty letters—begins in 1913 and ends more or less coincidentally soon after Sterling's death in late 1926. His passing marked an important juncture in the culture and history of that time. The Loveman and Smith exchange ended simply because circumstances of life and mundane work forced them to become preoccupied elsewise. Smith himself did not feel free to move elsewhere. He and his parents depended too much on each other as a basic family unit for Clark to move away at any real distance or for any long period.

We have probably underestimated the value of Smith's painting and pictorial sketches, but after the suave and high technical quality of his prose and poetry, this particular art of his has never "grabbed" or impressed us in spite of the occasional otherworldly landscape or daemonic head, plant, or other entity. It is a pity that he never found anyone—relative or friend—who could have taught him such techniques as he might have required.

The sculptures on the other hand succeed on their own terms. Whether created or "found" or discovered as a small piece of rock. They suggest an essence extending itself infinitely on into time and space. this is all the more noteworthy because most of them are small in scale. He did not manage to distribute these widely. Small rock or stone carvings (even talc) are easier to sculpt while holding a specimen of the mineral in the hand. They cost much more to mail (properly packaged) than letters or art sketches. Apparently he did sell quite a few by mail, above all to August Derleth. His descendants have a potential gold mine in his major collection.

We can wholeheartedly recommend this extraordinary volume to the keen student, the aficionado in depth, of both these poets, whether Loveman or Smith. These letters make up a vital part of both their biographies or autobiographies as it were. The book benefits hugely from the impeccable editing by Joshi and Schultz. The cover art and design by Jason van Hollander seems appropriately picturesque as well as discombobulated. Derrick Hussey as the publisher every kudos and compliment.

Phantasmascope

Donald Sidney-Fryer

SAMUEL LOVEMAN. *Out of the Immortal Night: Selected Works.* Edited by S. T. Joshi and David E. Schultz. New York: Hippocampus Press, 2nd edition 2021. 514 pp. $25.00 tpb.

Misleadingly marginal and solitary, the singular poet and author Samuel Loveman (1887–1976), *the* ultimate bibliophile, with much of his common oeuvre comes before us, relatively unknown and perhaps unknowable—apart from his close association with fabulist or fabulator H. P. Lovecraft and arch-poet Hart Crane. Thanks above all to Joshi and Schultz, Loveman stands restored to life as the literary creator.

Just as Schultz has brought back to general cognizance Leah Bodine Drake and her magnific and even larger tome (over 700 pages), Joshi and Schultz have done the same for Loveman, a no less deserving figure. This is an event long since overdue. Once again we owe all due credit to Joshi, Schultz, and publisher Derrick Hussey. Bravissimo!

We had not known of the first appearance of this volume in 2004, and that the exchange of letters between Loveman and Clark Ashton Smith (published as *Born under Saturn*) began in 1913 thanks to George Sterling and then terminated some time soon after the latter's death in late 1926. The correspondence, a major volume at over 500 pages, came out in August from Hippocampus Press.

Thus at long last we have Loveman with much of the appanage of his distinctive output, plus much biographical detail. Let us celebrate this rare phenomenon as it seems fitting and proper! But let us also review an appraise the weighty tome itself in the order of its carefully assembled contents.

Since Loveman (he admits it) did not take very good care of his writings—apart from some of his poetry, all the major works like *The Hermaphrodite* and the dialogue or drama *The Sphinx*—Joshi and Schultz have rendered a genuine service by preparing this volume. A listing of the major sections reveals an abundance of well-curated labor, sic:—

Introduction, by S. T. Joshi
 I. Poetry
   Poems (1911; 7 pieces)
   The Hermaphrodite and Other Poems (1936; 73 pieces)
   Uncollected Poems (91, covering much of his life and career—he
   lived to be almost 90)
 II. Drama (10 pieces)
 III. Translations (48, mostly from Heine, Baudelaire, and Verlaine)
 IV. Fiction (10 pieces)
 V. Nonfiction (67 miscellanea, including many reviews and many
   comments on other authors)
Appendix (11 pieces, miscellanea, including two major interviews with
   Loveman and several reviews of his work by other authors).

Let us read, nay peruse, these multifarious contents so that we can make apt comment in general and in detail. But let us not neglect to mention the enigmatic and intriguing cover art (1944): a sphinx! By William Sommer, as chosen by the publisher. The title of the collection overall appears equally well-chosen. It derives from the first line of *The Hermaphrodite*: "Out of the deep, immortal night." It is also a clue to the title of appraisal-essay, phantom or phantasm: these many people, many or most, as recalled or invoked by Loveman, are all now long deceased.

Between the introduction by Joshi and Schultz and the Appendix (compiled by divers hands), we learn much about Loveman's life and career, painstakingly researched and assembled. Let us re-read the poetry. We acknowledge and respect that Loveman is a consummate craftsman, using a variety of norms, forms, themes, meters, etc., including rime. He began in Cleveland, and after Hart Crane moved from there to New York City, in 1919, Loveman followed in November 1924, usually working as an erudite bookman in a variety of prominent bookstores in the Big City. He continued to write poetry more or less all his life.

Among other topics Loveman sings or celebrates single books and author-poets, and always and above all, the joys of art and literature. Apart from his acknowledged masterpieces the lack of secure detail in place or person—during almost 100 pieces (the uncollected poems)—makes the mindset or viewpoint at times undetermined or too vague. What is he discussing? While his technique is chaste and pure, we find perhaps too much reliance on gems and minerals to describe or suggest things non-jewel-like in his prose and poetry. But this is a minor complaint about style and presentation.

The next complaint is a major one. Where in the poetry is there a sense of urgency, any dramatic urgency? We also feel on occasion the lack of vivid imagery, quite a contrast to Clark Ashton Smith. Loveman was, at first, hostile to Walt Whitman but later waxed more sympathetic. As for us, we thank the gods of Olympus that dear old Walt came along and broke out of the too-confining corset of traditional poetry and of the slavish Graecophile. We say this in spite of Loveman's adherence to strict traditional prosody with meter and rime. His own poetic terrain appears to be some Greek mythological never-never land beyond the historical Hellas.

A major plus for us: he makes correct and consistent usage of the true second person singular: thou, thee, thy, thine. A pity that we can't revive it for everyday use except in an intimate context with lovers or close friends. It would seem that Loveman did not know Greek in depth. Why did he not save some money to go to Greece, if he was so enamoured of things Greek or Hellene? Modern Greece would not disappoint any more than does Ancient/Modern Egypt. The latter no longer speaks Hamitic, but Arab—except the Coptic liturgy recited in the same manner as the Arabic in the Mohammedan liturgy.

Although Loveman's pure poetry is presumably personal, he never or rarely makes reference even indirectly to his own homosexuality—despite the well-known fact of Greek Love then and now. Halfway through the dramatic dialogue *The Sphinx*, he grants us a piquant homosexual detail: "My eunuchs became abominable creatures with gigantic phalluses of black ivory." It appears like one of the extravagances of the *Arabian Nights* or the *History of the Caliph Vathek!*

We should mention the long nine-part monologue "Debs in Prison," anent Eugene Victor Debs (1855–1926), the early American socialist. He ranks among the first who felt compassion and pity for his fellow humans, those oppressed, manacled, suppressed, and imprisoned. Loveman's poem (Debs gives it as a soliloquy) becomes a disquisition about injustice.

Loveman's dramatic pieces include *The Sphinx* and nine single other dramatic scenes, which assembled in an artful way might constitute a worthwhile dramatic evening (two hours?) by one author, perhaps as mounted by some college's drama department. The scenes for plays by Shakespeare and others might also function as surreptitious additions to those texts; i.e., *King Lear* and *Macbeth*. Shakespeare himself might very well have welcomed their addition. He did collaborate with Marlowe and others.

The translations from Heine, Baudelaire, and Verlaine all seem well done, and do not appear like bald, literal renderings into English, but more like original and accomplished poems. The twenty-four pieces from Heine remind us how close he is to Poe, Baudelaire, and Smith.

The section devoted to fiction reveals just fewer than a dozen short stories. Several are tiny such as "Anteros" (of Samosata). The stories appear more or less as existential fables than conventional tales. "A Ruined Paradise": two canoeists become lost in a river's meandering sidestream and succumb to the effluvium (perfume) of some huge poppies along the shore. A true opioid. "The Faun": Pan is ill but Syrinx his young friend succors him and he recovers. This tale succeeds as a curious but charming fable.

"The Dog": this pitiful little tale "After the Russian" exposes a skinny and hungry canine. A student attempts to help by bringing him home, but his family refuses to take him in. Plan goes awry, and the dog remains hungry at the end, poor Kritter! "Ferris Thone": a tale somewhat autobiographical of Loveman as poet and bookseller, but after a certain Hesketh relates it, he reveals it is only a fabrication. Durn! "An Impression": a good, very brief mood-piece of two men walking at sunset after an all-day rain. "A Hopeless Love": about the love between the beggar Jehan and a young bride (not his). Another melancholy story of medieval Paris.

"The One Who Found Pity": one man kills another, but because he finds pity (supernatural?), many calamities come close but pass him by. The overall series of ten tales or sketches ends aptly with "Christmas Eve with Sherlock Holmes." Watson narrates, and once again the game's afoot! "The Adventure of the Runic Dagger"! These narratives reveal a firm and capable auctorial hand, but otherwise unremarkable.

Nonfiction. The biggest section of all (at over 100 pages). Here we learn a helluvalot about Loveman's tastes and preferences, all in line with what we know about him and his poetry. Loveman in one place directly confesses that he never took good care of the things he wrote. Which *is* a shame! This prose is as fascinating as his best poetry. But the collections of amateur journalism in various academic libraries proved an invaluable resource in finding and gathering the materials thus presented. Let the reader discover and explore this section by himself.

Following the section of nonfiction at 116 pages, the appendix is the largest at 91 pages and includes two interviews and several reviews done by other authors. The interview by John Unterecker (4 August 1962, 30 pages) covers much terrain cultural and literary. The other, "Conversations with Sam," conducted by Thomas J. Hubschman (c. 1964; 64 pages), covers even more terrain than Unterecker.

The second interviewer like the first used a tape recorder to record this enlightening interview. It includes a long section (at 22 pages) on Hart Crane. The latter led a very dissolute life involving too much alcohol and much homosexual action with young sailors that he picked up on the street or in neighborhood bars. They often robbed him. Crane strikes Hubschman "as an insufferable egotist," as he did others.

Also per the same interviewer, Loveman lightens his own melancholy at least once about the fate of his own poetry, stating, "It is just possible that someone will rediscover me." Loveman, in case we have not mentioned it before, reveals an acute sense of humor here and there but especially in his essay "Modern Poetry (An Exorcism)."

The Appendix ends with several small memoirs and a few brief reviews of *The Hermaphrodite,* ending with Benét's dismissive mention-appraisal. As this book of Loveman's demonstrates at length, he is much more than just "a pleasing poet." Loveman's hope about his own work has indeed found tangible realization. Messieurs Joshi, Schultz, and Hussey have in fact rediscovered him and his writings. Bravissimo to all three and to the poet himself.

Notes on Contributors

Manuel Arenas is a writer of verse and prose in the Gothic horror tradition. His work has appeared in *Spectral Realms* and *Penumbra*, from Hippocampus Press, and in sundry genre anthologies. He has recently released his first collection of prose and poetry, *Book of Shadows: Grim Tales and Gothic Fancies*, from Jackanapes Press. He currently resides in Phoenix, Arizona.

David Barker is coauthor of three books of Lovecraftian fiction with the late W. H. Pugmire: *The Revenant of Rebecca Pascal*, *In the Gulfs of Dream and Other Lovecraftian Tales*, and *Witches in Dreamland*. His collection of horror fiction, *Her Wan Embrace*, is due from Weird House in 2021, and his story "Who Maketh Fertile the Fields" appeared in *A Walk in a Darker Wood: An Anthology of Folk Horror* in 2020.

Benjamin Blake is the author of the novel *The Devil's Children*, the poetry collections *Standing on the Threshold of Madness*, *Southpaw Nights* (poetry and prose), *All the Feral Dogs of Los Angeles* (with Cole Bauer), *Dime Store Poetry*, and *Tenebrae in Aeternum* (published by Hippocampus Press).

Adam Bolivar is a poet of dark fantasy, a weird fiction writer, and a playwright for marionettes. He is the author of *The Lay of Old Hex* (Hippocampus Press), *The Ettinfell of Beacon Hill* (Jackanapes Press), and the forthcoming *Ballads for the Witching Hour* (Hippocampus Press). A native of Boston, he now resides in Portland, Oregon.

Frank Coffman is a retired professor of English and Creative Writing. He has published speculative poetry and short fiction in a variety of magazines, anthologies, and collections. His three collections of poetry are: *The Coven's Hornbook and Other Poems* (2019), *Black Flames and Gleaming Shadows* (2020), and *Eclipse of the Moon* (2021). His collection of seven occult detective mysteries, *Three against the Dark*, will be released this year.

Scott J. Couturier is a poet and prose writer of the weird, liminal, and darkly fantastic. His work has appeared in numerous venues, including *The Audient Void, Eye to the Telescope, The Dark Corner Zine, Space and Time,* and *Weirdbook.* Currently he works as a copy and content editor for Mission Point Press, living an obscure reverie in the wilds of northern Michigan with his partner/live-in editor and two cats. His debut short story collection, *The Box,* is due out in 2021 from Silent Motorist Media.

Along with previously in *Spectral Realms,* **Harris Coverley** has verse published or forthcoming in *Polu Texni, California Quarterly, Star*Line, Scifaikuest, Tales from the Moonlit Path, The Five-Two: Crime Poetry Weekly, View From Atlantis, Danse Macabre, Once Upon A Crocodile,* and many others. A former Rhysling nominee and member of the Weird Poets Society, he lives in Manchester, England.

Margaret Curtis (Master of Creative Arts, Grad. Dip. Transpersonal Breathwork, Dip. LIS), witch, writer, artist, healer and activist, lives in Wollongong, New South Wales, with her family and a black cat. Published in magazines and anthologies, in print and online, including *Midnight Echo* and *Spectral Realms,* she is the author of four collections of poetry, including *Voice of the Goddess and Other Poems* (1991).

Holly Day's poetry has recently appeared in *Asimov's Science Fiction, Grain,* and the *Tampa review.* Her newest poetry collections are *In This Place, She Is Her Own, A Wall to Protect Your Eyes, Where We Went Wrong,* and *Cross Referencing a Book of Summer,* while her newest nonfiction books are *Music Theory for Dummies* and *Tattoo FAQ.*

Melissa Ridley Elmes is a Virginia native currently living in Missouri in an apartment that delightfully approximates a hobbit hole. Her poetry and fiction have appeared in *Star*Line, Eye to the Telescope, In Parentheses, Gyroscope, Thimble, HeartWood,* and various other print and web venues, and her first collection of poems, *Arthurian Things,* was published by Dark Myth Publications in 2020.

Cataloging librarian **Adele Gardner** is an active member of HWA with a master's in English literature. She has published a poetry book (*Dreaming of Days in Astophel*) and more than 400 poems, stories, art, and essays in

Flame Tree's *Lost Souls* and *Haunted House* anthologies, Strange *Horizons*, *NewMyths.com*, *Mythic Delirium*, *Horror Garage* (Paula Guran), and more. She curated the SFPA 2019 Halloween Poetry Reading (sfpoetry.com/halloween.html).

Wade German is the author of the poetry collections *Dreams from a Black Nebula* (Hippocampus Press) and *The Ladies of the Everlasting Lichen and Other Relics* (Mount Abraxas Press), the verse drama *Children of Hypnos*, and three slim volumes of verse in Portuguese translation, *Incantations*, *Apparitions*, and *Phantasmagorias* (Raphus Press).

Thomas Goff is the 2021 winner of the Robinson Jeffers Tor House Prize for poetry, with his poem "'Blind Tom's' *Battle of Manassas*." He is finishing a new poetry collection, *Reading in the Dark*, partly on the pandemic experience, partly on the authorship of Shakespeare, with occasional forays into the occult.

Maxwell I. Gold is a Rhysling Award-nominated author of weird fiction, writing short stories and prose poems that center upon his profane Cyber Gods Mythos. His work has appeared in numerous publications including *The Audient Void, Space and Time, Weirdbook,* and many others.

P. B. Grant hails from Scotland and currently lives in Nova Scotia, Canada. His poetry, essays, and articles have been widely published in a variety of books and journals.

Christine Irving is an eclectic poet with an abiding interest in symbolism, myth, and the occult. Though her writing tends to remain mostly in the upper realms, she is well aware of the necessity, beauty, and balance of the dark. Her work consists of making connections between seemingly disparate happenings, places, and things. Her work often combines the mythical and elusive with the ordinary and concrete.

Lori R. Lopez is a quirky author, illustrator, poet, and songwriter who likes to wear hats. Her Gothic-toned and generous poetry collection *Darkverse: The Shadow Hours* was nominated for the 2018 Elgin Award, while individual poems have been nominated for Rhysling Awards.

Stories and verse have appeared in numerous publications. Other titles include *The Dark Mister Snark, Leery Lane,* and *An Ill Wind Blows.*

Native New Yorker **LindaAnn LoSchiavo,** recently Poetry SuperHighway's Poet of the Week, is a member of SFPA and the Dramatists Guild. Elgin Award winner *A Route Obscure and Lonely* and *Concupiscent Consumption* are her latest poetry titles. Forthcoming is a paranormal poetry collection, a collaborative horror chapbook, and an Italian-centric book inspired by her Aeolian Island heritage. She has been leading a poetry critique group for two years.

Charles Lovecraft studies English at Macquarie University, Sydney. His main literary and life influences have been H. P. Lovecraft and macabre literature. More than 150 of his poems have been published. As publisher-editor he runs weird poetry imprint P'rea Press (www.preapress.com). He is working on a long Lovecraftian weird poem, *The Caller of Darkness,* and has edited thirty-four books.

Mack W. Mani is an award-winning screenwriter, poet, and author. His work has appeared in *Strange Horizons, NewMyths,* and the *Pedestal Magazine.* In 2018 he won Best Screenplay at the H. P. Lovecraft Film Festival. He currently lives in Portland, Oregon.

Kurt Newton's most recent poetry appearances include *Spectral Realms, Eye to the Telescope, Cosmic Horror Monthly, Crow Toes Quarterly,* and *Penumbric.* He is the author of eight collections of poetry. His ninth collection, *Songs of the Underland & Other Macabre Machinations,* will be published in 2022 by Ravens Quoth Press.

Ngo Binh Anh Khoa is a teacher of English in Ho Chi Minh City, Vietnam. In his free time, he enjoys daydreaming, reading, and occasionally writing poetry for personal entertainment. His speculative poems have appeared in NewMyths.com, *Heroic Fantasy Quarterly, The Audient Void,* and other venues.

Manuel Pérez-Campos's poetry has appeared previously in *Spectral Realms* and *Weird Fiction Review.* A collection of his poetry in the key of the weird is in progress; so is a collection of ground-breaking essays on H. P. Lovecraft. He lives in Bayamón, Puerto Rico.

Carl E. Reed is showroom manager for a window, siding, and door company just outside Chicago. Former jobs include U.S. marine, long-haul trucker, improvisational actor, cab driver, security guard, bus driver, door-to-door encyclopedia salesman, construction worker, and art show MC. His poetry has been published in the *Iconoclast* and *Spectral Realms*; short stories in *Black Gate* and *newWitch* magazines.

Geoffrey Reiter is Associate Professor and Coordinator of Literature at Lancaster Bible College. He is also an Associate Editor at the website Christ and Pop Culture, where he frequently writes about weird horror and dark fantasy. As a scholar of weird fiction, Reiter has published academic articles on such authors as Arthur Machen, Bram Stoker, Clark Ashton Smith, and William Peter Blatty.

Ann K. Schwader lives and writes in Colorado. Her newest collection, *Unquiet Stars*, is now out from Weird House Press. Two of her earlier collections, *Wild Hunt of the Stars* (Sam's Dot, 2010) and *Dark Energies* (P'rea Press, 2015), were Bram Stoker Award Finalists. In 2018, she received the Science Fiction & Fantasy Poetry Association's Grand Master award. She is also a two-time Rhysling Award winner.

Darrell Schweitzer has finally gotten his overdue third collection of poetry. *Dancing Before Azathoth* will be published soon by P'rea Press, with an introduction by S. T. Joshi. His other two poetry collections are *Groping toward the Light* (2002) and *Ghosts of Past and Future* (2010), both available from Wildside Press. His ambition is to be one day better known for these than for rhyming Cthulhu in a limerick. He is otherwise a short-story writer, novelist, essayist, anthologist, and a former editor of *Weird Tales*.

Donald Sidney-Fryer is the author of *Emperor of Dreams: A Clark Ashton Smith Bibliography* (Donald M. Grant, 1978), *The Atlantis Fragments* (Hippocampus Press, 2009), and many other volumes. He has edited Smith's *Poems in Prose* (Arkham House, 1965) and written many books and articles on California poets. His autobiography *Hobgoblin Apollo*

(2016) and volumes of miscellany, most recently *Random Notes, Random Lines* (2021), have been published by Hippocampus Press.

Claire Smith writes poetry about other worlds. Her work regularly appears in *Spectral Realms*. Most recently her poems have also featured in *Songs of Eretz, Corvid Queen, Illumen,* and *Sage Cigarettes*. She holds an M.A. in English from the Open University and is currently studying for a Ph.D. at the University of Gloucestershire. Claire lives in Gloucestershire with her husband and their very spoiled Tonkinese cat, Ishtar.

Oliver Smith is a visual artist and writer from Cheltenham, UK. His poetry has appeared in *Mirror Dance, Dreams & Nightmares, Rivet, Strange Horizons, Liminality,* and *Penumbric*. Oliver was awarded first place in the BSFS 2019 competition for his poem "Better Living through Witchcraft," and his poem "Lost Palace, Lighted Tracks" was nominated for the 2020 Pushcart Prize. In 2020 he was awarded a Ph.D. in Literary and Critical Studies.

Christina Sng is the two-time Bram Stoker Award–winning author of *A Collection of Dreamscapes* (2020) and *A Collection of Nightmares* (2017). Her poetry, fiction, essays, and art have appeared in numerous venues worldwide, including *Fantastic Stories of the Imagination, Interstellar Flight Magazine, Penumbric, Southwest Review,* and the *Washington Post*.

DJ Tyrer is the person behind Atlantean Publishing and has been published in *The Rhysling Anthology*, issues of *Cyäegha, The Horrorzine, Scifaikuest, Sirens Call, Star*Line, Tigershark,* and *The Yellow Zine*. The echapbook *One Vision* is available from Tigershark Publishing. *SuperTrump* and *A Wuhan Whodunnit* are available for download from Atlantean Publishing.

Steven Withrow's most recent verse collection is *The Bedlam Philharmonic*. His poems appear in *Spectral Realms, Asimov's Science Fiction,* and *Dreams & Nightmares*. His short poem "The Sun Ships," from a collection of the same title, was nominated for a 2016 Rhysling Award from the Science Fiction & Fantasy Poetry Association. He lives in Falmouth, Massachusetts.

Jordan Zuniga is an emerging Christian creative writer who actively writes and promotes on Instagram @cccreativewriter and on vocal.media as Jordan Zuniga. He enjoys writing high fantasy (sometimes a little dark for some Christian audiences) and speculative fiction. He has appearances with *Spectral Realms, Christiandevotions.us, Poetry Coloring Book: Halloween Edition,* and *Literary Yard* magazine.

www.ingramcontent.com/pod-product-compliance
Lightning Source LLC
Chambersburg PA
CBHW060806050426
42449CB00008B/1558